Christianity and War
in a Nuclear Age

Books by Richard Harries

Prayers of Hope
Turning to Prayer
Prayers of Grief and Glory
Being a Christian
Should a Christian support Guerillas?
Praying round the Clock
The Authority of Divine Love
Seasons of the Spirit

(with George Every and Kallistos Ware)
Prayer and the Pursuit of Happiness
Morning has Broken

Edited and contributed to

What Hope in an Armed World?
Reinhold Niebuhr and the Issues of our Time

Contributed to

Stewards of the Mysteries of God
ed. E. James
Unholy Warfare
ed. D. Martin and P. Mullen
The Cross and the Bomb
ed. F. Bridger
Dropping the Bomb
ed. J. Gladwyn
Julian, Woman of our Time
ed. R. Llewellyn
If Christ be not raised
ed. J. Greenhalgh

Christianity and War in a Nuclear Age

by

RICHARD HARRIES

Dean of King's College, London

MOWBRAY
LONDON & OXFORD

FOR DAVID AND NATASHA

ISBN 0 264 67053 1

First published 1986
by A.R. Mowbray & Co. Ltd,
Saint Thomas House, Becket Street,
Oxford, OX1 1SJ

Typeset by Dentset, 35 St Clements, Oxford, OX4 1AB.
Printed in Great Britain by Biddles Ltd., Guildford.

British Library Cataloguing in Publication Data
Harries, Richard, *1936–*
    Christianity and war in a nuclear age.
    1. Nuclear warfare—Religious aspects—Christianity
    I. Title
    261.8'73   BR115.A85

ISBN 0 264 67053 1

Contents

Acknowledgements

I am extremely grateful to Dr Sydney Bailey, the Reverend Dr Anthony Harvey, Dr Barrie Paskins, Sir Michael Quinlan, Dr Anthony Sivers and the Reverend Professor Keith Ward who kindly read the typescript and made a number of valuable comments. I would also like to thank Gill Ryeland and Carolyn Adams for kindly typing the book.

CHAPTER ONE

Love and force

'We must love one another or die'. wrote W. H. Auden in a famous poem.[1] Auden later came to regret that line, considering it sentimental, on the grounds that 'we all die anyway'. Nevertheless, a line that widely caught the mood of a previous generation is even more apposite in our own nuclear age. We must love one another. Moreover, whatever else Christians might disagree about, on this at least they are agreed: love is at the heart of the Christian life. The Christian ethic is a love ethic.

The idea of shooting at someone seems clearly contrary to love. If this is what we feel about harming a single individual, the thought of turning a key that will release a missile and bring death to hundreds of thousands and perhaps millions, cannot fail to arouse a sense of horror and revulsion in all of us. Yet feelings alone are not enough. On this subject above all, where so much emotion is rightly aroused, it is necessary to think clearly. For what is it to love? There is a tendency amongst some Christians to bring the word love into the debate as though this, in itself, was an answer to all the questions at issue. However, as Professor Basil Mitchell has written:

> Love ensures that the only question before the lover's mind is: 'what can I do to help?' It does not answer that question. To answer it requires moral insight and to say this is to re-open all the controversies that moral philosophers have engaged in.[2]

'This is to re-open all the controversies that moral philosophers have engaged in.' These are words that need to be heeded. Preachers, moralists and would-be prophets will no doubt continue to use the word love to move their listeners in

1

a predetermined direction: but the questioning mind, that is, the ordinary, honest human mind, will still ask, 'What *is* the most loving action? I want to love: but what does love dictate?'

The Christian concept of love is rich and fathomless because it is ultimately grounded in the mutual giving and receiving of the blessed Trinity. Nevertheless, all Christians would agree that any concept of love worthy of the name must at least include wanting the good of the other person. Love involves more than this, and it certainly includes a willingness to receive from the other as well as give to them, but this at least is involved. To love someone, as Professor Mitchell puts it, is to have in the forefront of our mind the question, 'what can I do to help?' It means therefore having a fundamental good-will towards that person: wanting their well-being. To love involves, as a minimum, wanting the good of others. But this is to begin the debate, not close it.

The first fact that has to be faced is that in many contexts we are required to love not a single neighbour in a face-to-face relationship, but a multiplicity of neighbours. This means that as often as not love involves assessing and discriminating between a variety of sometimes conflicting claims. On some occasions these claims can be, if not fully met, at least resolved to everyone's satisfaction on the basis of equal distribution. In a family of four, all of whom have normal appetites, the apple pie is divided into quarters. Even in a family, however, it is rarely as simple as this. One child might be extra hungry or another might need extra spoiling. Outside the family, in the wider community, there are almost always competing claims to consider, where a decision in favour of one person or group leads to the relative disadvantage of others. For example, conservation interests recently arranged for the release of seventy sea eagles, an endangered species, in the north of Scotland. Landowners then complained that the eagles ate the sheep and made it even more difficult for crofters to eke out their very precarious living in those parts. In the National Health Service, with its limited resources, hard decisions are having to be made every day. For a decision in favour of one group leads inevitably to prolonged discomfort and even death in other groups. People die because of lack of kidney machines. Old people and the mentally ill suffer because they do not have all the provision that would be made available to them in a world of unlimited resources. Loving almost always means making hard decisions. It may mean choosing between the potential intimidation of a legitimate picket line and the potential violence of an authorized police riot squad. It may mean deciding between the life of the gunman holding up a post office and the life of a postmistress behind the counter.

Too much talk about love assumes a one-to-one relationship. But we do not live on an isolated island with just one other person. We live in a human society with many people all of whom make a claim of some kind upon us. That is the first point. The second is that it is by no means obvious, even in a one-to-one relationship, in what the good of the other person consists. In general, our understanding of another person's good depends in large measure on the person we ourselves are, on our fundamental values and assumptions. It is natural for two parents, who are both professional musicians, to want their children to develop all the musical ability they have within them. Another person, who spends most of his life in a pub, may ask no more of a friend than that he becomes a good drinking companion. A heroin addict simply may not care whether other people become addicts. On the other hand most parents, when they reflect on 'the good' of their children, think not only of the basic necessities of life, a fulfilling job and a stable, loving marriage. In addition, and perhaps before anything else, they will want their children to have a character that can be respected. They want their children to grow up to be decent people. Their understanding of the good includes moral as well as material considerations. It is not therefore surprising that our 'good', according to the Christian faith, is a rich and distinctive notion. It refers not simply to individual well-being but to our well-being in community. It refers not only to our well-being on this earth but to our eternal happiness in heaven. It refers not only to the natural flowering of our potential for creative work and loving, human relationships, but also to our capacity to love God and to love others as God himself loves us. All this has to be taken into account when we are trying to work out what it means to love and what might be the relationship between love and force.

Christ bids us love not only like-minded people but those who are indifferent or hostile to us. This is fundamental to a Christian view of existence and no believer can ignore it.

> You have heard that they were told, 'Love your neighbours, hate your enemy'. But what I tell you is this: Love your enemies and pray for your persecutors; only so can you be children of your heavenly Father, who makes his sun rise on good and bad alike, and sends rain on the honest and dishonest.[3]

To love our enemies is to have a genuine good-will towards them, to wish them well, to desire their good. But what is this good? It is sometimes stated, as though it were a self-evident truth, that love of enemy and not resisting an enemy are synonymous. But can it really be in the best interests of a bully to be allowed to get away with his bullying? St Augustine wrote:

> He whose freedom to do wrong is taken away suffers a useful form of restraint, since nothing is more unfortunate than the good fortune of sinners, who grow bold by not being punished — a penalty in itself — and whose evil will is strengthened by the enemy within.[4]

The first step in loving a bully or a criminal therefore is to stop him in his tracks. This brings home to them the fact that bullying and crime do not pay. It stops the evil tendency within being strengthened by success. Nevertheless, though this is true, our deepest suspicions are aroused by this whole line of thought. We have heard too many cruel parodies of the theme, 'This is for your own good'. Excessive corporal punishment and even torture have sometimes been justified on the grounds that it is done for the good of the other person. Further, it has to be admitted that some of St Augustine's language sounds harsh to our softer age. But those who have, for example, administered excessive corporal punishment with a spurious justification have erred not in talking about the good of the person punished or in thinking that it might be right sometimes to punish, but in over-estimating the good-will in themselves and being blind to the extent that personal animosity, unconscious rage and vindictiveness can enter into such actions. That is why St Augustine urged the cultivation of a Christian inner disposition even in war, while at the same time stressing that a war could be waged with love.

> Therefore, these precepts of patience are always to be preserved in the heart, to keep it in readiness, and those kindly feelings which keep us from returning evil for evil are always to be developed in the will. But, we often have to act with a sort of kindly harshness, when we are trying to make unwilling souls yield, because we have to consider their welfare rather than their inclination, . . . in punishing a son, however harshly, a father's love is certainly not cast aside . . . Thus, if the earthly state observes those Christian teachings, even war will not be waged without kindness, and it will be easier for a society whose peace is based on piety and justice to take thought for the conquered.[5]

However often restraining force has revealed a spirit of vengeance rather than a spirit of reconciliation, it can in principle express an attitude of love and be directed towards the good of the other person. It can be an act of love. We do not doubt that when a parent forcibly prevents a child from cycling at night without lights, this is an act of love concerned with the child's safety. We do not doubt that when a policeman apprehends a drunken driver this act is, similarly, for his own good as well as the good of other people whom he is in danger of injuring. Nor need we doubt that love can be the motive even when the use of force is much more severe.

The relationship between love and restraining force rests on the fact that actions have consequences. It is fundamental to moral action that we should be able, to some extent, to predict the consequences of our action and take them into account. Moral decision making requires that we try to assess the probable consequences of different courses of action and choose in the light of our predictions. Furthermore, it is required of us as human beings that we accept the consequences of our actions. In an ideal world, a universe that was totally transparent to the good, good actions would lead to good consequences not only for others but for the doer of the action. They would flourish in every sense of the word. Bad actions, by contrast, would lead not so much to harmful consequences for others, as they do now, but to the personal diminishment of the doer of the action. The world in which we actually live, however, is not like that. Often other people suffer because of us and we suffer because of others. The innocent are hurt and the wicked prosper. This lament is at the heart of the Old Testament. But it will not always be so. For we live, despite appearances, in a moral universe, one which is on the side of value. In the end goodness will out and be revealed in all its glory.

When 'God is all in all' inner disposition, outward action and the total state of affairs will all be of a piece. This means that there is an intrinsic connection or nexus between decisions and consequences for the decider. Thus, when a bully is stopped in his tracks or a criminal stockbroker is arrested, this is not only for the protection of society but for his own good. The consequences of his actions are brought home to him. He experiences a foretaste of that final state of affairs in which the good person flourishes and the evil person withers.

This gives him the opportunity to realize that he is a moral being, to accept what has happened as just, and live in a different way. To treat a wrongdoer entirely as a sick person is a failure of love, in that it is a fundamental denial of his dignity as a moral human being. Apprehending wrongdoers brings it home to them that they live in a moral universe, and that they themselves are moral beings with the opportunity to change their outlook and live in a new way.

Restraining force can and ought to be the expression of good-will, directed towards the good of those who are restrained as well as the good of society as a whole. The personal limitations and weaknesses of those who have the responsibility of exercising restraining force are always likely to distort their actions. Public servants, the police and the armed forces are all governed by strict codes of conduct which are both legal and customary. These professional codes of conduct result from the combination of two factors: restraining force is intended to be the expression of good-will, but because of human weaknesses it will never be simply this. Professionalism seeks to minimize personal feelings of animosity, greed, sadism and so on, and encourages legal, rational, objective action, which is the form love takes for a public servant in a public role.

Ronald Sider and Richard Taylor in *Nuclear Holocaust and Christian Hope* agree that coercive discipline can be the expression of love, and admit that such discipline is essential, not only in family life but also in society. They draw the line, however, at the use of armed force. They maintain that love is fully compatible with economic boycott, prophetic condemnation and political pressure:

> But it is not compatible with lethal violence. In the former cases, one can genuinely love the other person and call on him as a free person to repent and change, but it makes no sense to call a person to repentance as you put a bullet through his head.[6]

This is an interesting and powerful challenge, to which three points can be made. First, 'shoot to kill' is not a Christian maxim. The purpose of armed force is to render the attacker harmless. Even in war, when it is highly likely that a number of people will be killed in a particular attack, killing is not the objective. In police work, even when the police are armed, the police will normally be able to disable a gunman temporarily rather than kill him. Secondly, the idea that repentance is possible only on this earth is not shared by all Christians. An alternative view is that God, in his mercy, continues to confront us with his truth and love even after death. In William Golding's phrase, the lightning of God's love wears away at the pincer-like claws of our egotism with a compassion that is 'timeless and without mercy'.[7] Thirdly, as already stated, there are innumerable conflict situations in which it is simply not posssible to maximize the good of all involved. We have to choose between two lesser goods or even two evils. The police may have to choose between the life of a deranged assassin spraying bullets into a crowded department store and the lives of the harmless shoppers. So, contrary to Sider and Taylor, it is possible to shoot and love at the same time. If love is conceived primarily in emotional terms, of course, this is not true. In order to shoot, a policeman or soldier has to act with a professional detachment, an apparent hardness. This is the only way in which he can do his job. But this professionalism does not rule out a fundamental attitude of good-will towards the assailant.

This assertion can be tested out in two examples. One of the strongest and in some ways purest of human loves can be that of a father for his son. In a European country before the second World War, one young man, dearly loved by his father, joins a Nazi group. The father, bitterly opposed to Nazi ideas, joins the resistance struggle and in the subsequent fighting finds that he has killed his son. The father's heart is rent with all the anguish of David's lament, 'O my son Absalom, my son, my son Absalom! Would God I had died for thee'.[8] Yet, if forced to choose, he would do the same again. Nazi ideas, for him, represent a denial of all that it means to be human. So although he does not blame his son for being caught up in them, through a combination of naïvety and misplaced idealism, he would still fight such ideas to the death, even if it certainly resulted in the death of his son.

Another example concerns a mother of three girls and their father who is suffering from a psychotic illness. In his deranged state he believes he must kill his wife and children in order to stop them suffering any more in this terrible world. The mother realizes what is happening and in the desperate struggle to protect her children kills her husband. She has not ceased to love him. Her heart is full of pity and anguish. But she knows that what she did was right, not simply from the point of view of her children but from that of her husband as well. For she knows that in his right mind he would be horrified at his action when insane, and would rather himself be killed than be responsible for the deaths of his wife and children. Similarly, in the first example, the father believes that if his son had a chance to see Nazi ideas for what they were, rather than through a false romantic haze, he would come to his senses and be appalled at what his gullibility had led him into.

Love is not incompatible with the use of restraining force. Nevertheless, there are many who would concede the points so far made whilst arguing that force used by one state against another is of a totally different order. 'Police work is radically different from warfare', write Sider and Taylor.[9] It is easy to understand this point of view for the following reasons. First, the question of scale. The number of people killed by the police, even in a country as violent as the United States, is tiny compared to the number that would be killed in a major war. Secondly, there is the indiscriminate nature of modern war. On the whole, when police shoot at armed criminals they can do so without hurting bystanders. In a European war, civilian casualties would be enormous. Thirdly, the question of justice in war always seems to confused. Within a state there is a final authority that can arbitrate on disputes. On the international scene, because there is no central authority with enough power to enforce its decisions, each country has to act as prosecutor, judge and law enforcement officer in its own cause. Fourthly, even a cursory reading of history reveals how states are inclined to use foreign policy issues as a means of taking the tension out of internal unrest. Fifthly, the propaganda power of the modern state is frightening. A state can easily convince its citizens about the justice of a cause which the citizens have not had adequate time or opportunity to examine.

These considerations combine to produce a frightening picture of the government of a modern state, for its own internal political reasons, using the full panoply of state propaganda to take its people into a war which would be grossly disproportionate to any possible end and which would result in huge numbers of civilian deaths.

For these, and other reasons, the view that there is a radical difference between the restraining force used by police and force used by the military, is a compelling one. However, such a view has itself to face grave objections that are not always considered as seriously as they should be. The

difficulty can be seen by the use of another example. A family
in which there is a good atmosphere of ordered love finds
itself in a wider community of total lawlessness. Authority
has completely broken down and there are no police. The
result is that gangs of marauding youths rampage round the
district, looting, raping and brutalizing anyone who gets in
their way. In order to protect themselves and wrest a
minimum social order out of the chaos a number of families
band together to protect one another. They become, in effect,
an unofficial police force. Gradually they bring the district
under control and break up the gangs. What this situation
makes clear is that it is impossible to have a civilized family
life in the midst of a wider community characterized by total
anarchy. For that anarchy would enter into every corner of
the society; nothing would be safe. Furthermore, where there
is such anarchy, those conscious of a responsibility to combat
it have to take action themselves. They do so in the name of a
moral authority which is higher than any political authority
and which exists even when the normal political authority has
been destroyed. Similarly, on the international scene. It is an
illusion to think that a country can concentrate on achieving a
civilized social life within its own borders whilst being totally
detached from what goes on outside them. For if what goes
on outside is anarchy, with the most ruthless countries
expanding where they can and taking what they can, then no
country would be safe for long.

This point is rooted in theological truth. If it is God's will
that we co-operate with him in maintaining the conditions
without which no human society can exist, a point which will
be considered further in a subsequent chapter, then this must
apply equally to both civil and international society. The
ultimate justification for any kind of police work is that
through such restraining force the conditions of *pax-ordo-
iustitia,* necessary for the development of human lives, are
achieved; and as it is God's purpose to bring about rational
beings it is also his purpose, as an essential precondition, to
bring about the conditions to make this possible. It would be
contradictory for a Christian to co-operate with God in
upholding the moral law within a country, whilst being
indifferent to all the violations of that moral law outside its

own borders. To believe in the just use of police force, whilst denying the right of the state to defend itself and its allies, is both illogical and an abrogation of responsibility; a refusal to co-operate with God in upholding the moral law.

This is in no way to minimize the difficulties for anyone who still believes that it may be a Christian duty to exercise restraining force on the international scene. Two of the major difficulties, the extent of the suffering likely to be caused by a modern war and its indiscriminate nature, will be considered in later chapters. It could be that, on the basis of the considerations in those chapters, a Christian will have to say that the difference between police work and military activity today is so vast that there is a difference not simply of degree but of kind; so that whilst the one can be supported the other cannot. Nevertheless, if that position were finally adopted, it still faces the difficulty just mentioned, which has both a practical and a theological cutting edge. From a practical point of view, would it ever be possible to find a harbour of civilized life in a gale of brutal and unrestrained anarchy? From a theological point of view, could it ever be right to refuse to co-operate with God in trying to uphold justice and the moral norms upon which society is based, however confused and terrifying the circumstances in which we might have to try to do this?

This chapter began with the assumption that all Christians are concerned to ground what they do in love. But love, considered as good-will directed towards the good of other people, is related to fundamental beliefs about the nature and destiny of man.[10] The command to love our enemy was considered and it was argued that this may involve resisting, *for his sake,* the unjust aggression he is seeking to perpetrate. Finally, it was admitted that whilst the use of force by the police might be seen as an act of love, it was difficult to conceive of modern war as such. However, whilst a fuller consideration of this must be left for later chapters, it was suggested that both on practical and theological grounds a Christian can hardly rest content with a system of *total* anarchy; as opposed to the tempered anarchy we have at present.

However, it may be maintained that Jesus has given a quite

specific content to the notion of love, one which rules out any resort to armed force. Love is not only good-will directed to the good of the other person or persons. Jesus has revealed what actions are, and what actions are not, compatible with such love. In principle, force can be used as an expression of love; for the good of the person towards whom it is directed. But suppose Jesus has forbidden the use of force as incompatible with love? To this argument we now turn.

Notes

1. 'September 1939' in *The English Auden,* ed E. Mendelson, Faber, 1977, p.245.
2. Basil Mitchell 'Ideals, Roles and Rules' in *Norm and Context in Christian Ethics,* ed Gene Outka and Paul Ramsey, SCM, 1969, p.353.
3. Matthew 5. 43-5.
4. St Augustine, Letter 138 to Marcellinus, *Letters* Volume 3, The Catholic University of America Press, 1953, p.47.
5. Ibid.
6. Ronald J. Sider and Richard K Taylor, *Nuclear Holocaust and Christian Hope,* Hodder and Stoughton, 1983, p.389.
7. William Golding, *Pincher Martin,* Penguin, 1956, p.184.
8. 2 Samuel 18.33.
9. *Nuclear Holocaust and Christian Hope,* p.389.
10. I addressed some of the issues of this chapter in 'Power, Coercion and Morality' in *The Cross and the Bomb,* ed. Francis Bridger, Mowbray, 1984, pp.69-90.

CHAPTER TWO

The teaching and example of Jesus

The claim of the Christian pacifist is that the content of love, what love requires of us, is made quite explicit in the teaching and example of Jesus. The teaching of Jesus in the sermon on the mount and his own example of going to the cross, leave no room for doubt: force is ruled out. The command to love our enemies, by itself, may not inexorably lead to pacifist conclusions. Nevertheless, taken with the examples given in the passage preceding the command, it could be held to do so.

> You have heard that it was said, 'An eye for an eye and a tooth for a tooth.' But I say to you, Do not resist one who is evil. But if any one strikes you on the right cheek, turn to him the other also; and if any one would sue you and take your coat, let him have your cloak as well; and if any one forces you to go one mile, go with him two miles. Give to him who begs from you, and do not refuse him who would borrow from you.[1]

All Christian scholars agree that Christ was not a legalist. He did not lay down detailed guidance for every conceivable situation that we might encounter. That was the tendency of the later Jewish Torah. The Torah was a comprehensive collection of rulings, covering multiple aspects of life, comparable more to the British legal system than to a contemporary book on moral theology. Jesus did not attempt to offer an alternative system of detailed legislation. His teaching in the sermon on the mount should not therefore be interpreted as though it had to be acted on according to the letter. This would be clearly contrary to his intention. Rather in C.H. Dodd's words, the examples in the sermon on the mount give us 'the quality and direction' of the actions required of us in a whole range of situations. Acting according to the letter can only lead to absurd conclusions, as was well brought out by P.G. Wodehouse. In one of his stories, a character called Battling Bilson is hit on the cheek, so, following the precepts of the sermon on the mount, he turns the other one. This too was struck, whereupon Battling Bilson knocked his opponent to the floor on the grounds that 'we only have two cheeks'.

Two other points need to be noticed about the examples given in Matthew 5. 38-42. First, none of them deal with a direct threat to life. Indeed the first example refers to an insult rather than a heavy blow. On the assumption that most people are right handed, we can only be struck on our right cheek by the back of another person's hand. This was a recognized insult. Secondly, all the examples refer to an action against the reader (originally the hearer). They do not tell us how we are to react if the injury is about to be inflicted on a person for whom the hearer is responsible, on a child, for example, or an old person. The significance of this passage is therefore less wide-reaching than is sometimes assumed. It deals only with relatively minor injuries to the person addressed. It does not consider direct threats to the life of someone for whom we are responsible.

There is of course a great deal of other material, both in the New Testament and the Old, that bears upon the morality of force, but the evidence has been very variously interpreted both to support a pacifist and a non-pacifist position. This famous passage has been singled out as it is a crux and because this more than any other text is used to show that, quite unambiguously, Jesus taught pacifism. But even this passage does not do that. In any case the exercise of appealing to particular texts in the Bible to prove a case, as pacifists and non-pacifists have done over the centuries, is of only limited value. Too much of this text-citing, even today, ignores the much more fundamental and difficult question of how the ethical teaching of Jesus is to be considered in relation to his message and mission as a whole.

All New Testament scholars agree that at the heart of the teaching of Jesus is his message about the kingdom of God. This is not just an inner state but life as a whole transformed and flourishing as God intends it to be. Throughout the Old

Testament people looked forward to the reign of God on earth, to the time when life in all its aspects, political, social and personal, would blossom and be totally translucent to the divine glory that is in and through all things. The message of Jesus is that in some decisive sense this longed-for time, this rule of God in the environment and in human affairs, is breaking into the present order through his words and actions. The sick were healed, demons cast out, the dead raised, lives transformed; all signs of the presence of this kingdom. The ethical teaching of Jesus is integrally related to this proclamation of the kingdom and any attempt to treat it in isolation misses the point. But how is it related? A variety of answers have been suggested but perhaps the simplest of all is the most convincing. This suggests that Jesus's teaching about the kingdom and the ethical claims that he put before people belong together as two sides of the same coin. For a person's attitude towards us cannot be separated from the expectations they have of us and the demands that they make upon us, and those will be integrally related to the kind of person they are. As was suggested in Chapter One, a person who spends most of his time in a pub will ask of a friend no more than that he be a good drinking companion. On the other hand, most parents care very much that their children grow up not only to do well in worldly terms, but also that they grow up with a moral character that can be respected. Because most parents love their children, what they expect of them, the moral ideal they have for them, is high. We cannot separate a person's presence with us from what they want of us, and what they want of us will reflect their own character and the depth of their care for us. If they care little they won't mind if, morally, we go to pieces. If they care much, they will care that we grow as a person. If a father is indifferent to his children, he is indifferent in two ways. He does nothing *for* them, and he expects nothing *of* them. On the other hand, a father who cares both does things for his children and wants them to realize their potential. This 'wanting' is experienced by the children as a kind of unseen pressure that is both expectation and claim. But, except when a father is living his own unfulfilled ambitions through his children, this 'wanting' is one essential aspect of a total love. God, who is perfect love, and who has made us in his own image, wants us to develop our capacity to love as he loves us. So we cannot know the love of God for us without at the same time knowing the expectation he has of us and the claim he makes upon us to love as he loves. The two belong together. His love for us is also a love which claims us for love. Jesus proclaimed the presence of this kingdom of love. He did not simply teach people about the nature of God's rule. He taught that this rule was, here and now, breaking into human life. He put both its grace and claims before people and called them to live in this realm, in God's presence, now.

Jesus taught people that the long-awaited kingdom of God was here. This kingdom is nothing less than the presence and rule of God himself. Jesus summoned people to live in this presence, which is love, and under this rule, which is love. For the love which is God's presence and the imperative to love are two aspects of the same reality. Thus the sublime teaching of Jesus about the love of God given in such parables as the lost sheep and the prodigal son, and his ethical teaching that we are to love without limit, are two aspects of the same reality. Both are rooted in and spring from the divine love incarnate, the one in whom the presence and rule of God are manifest.

How should we relate these claims to the routine responsibilities and duties of everyday life? It could be likened to the situation of a very old friend, whom we have not seen for years, ringing up from abroad to say he is arriving home tomorrow and much wants to see us. In the light of this we decide to take a day off from work and make our excuses at a social engagement. In the light of the presence of the kingdom our priorities are reordered. Everything looks different and is different. But, suppose our friend later rings up to say that his trip has to be postponed for two weeks. Most of us would take up our normal routine again. We would not usually take two weeks off work waiting for our friend to arrive. We have a living to earn and commitments to fulfil. The whole New Testament reflects a situation of postponement. In some decisive sense the rule of God has been established on earth in and through the person of Christ. Yet he himself taught a future consummation of this kingdom; indeed some scholars would say that his stress falls on this future. Then, after the death and resurrection of Christ, Christians associated this future consummation with the return of Christ in judgement and glory. Some parts of the New Testament reflect a belief in his imminent return. Other parts, which emphasize what he has already achieved, still look forward to the completion of his work. This tension between the inauguration of the reign of God on earth in Christ's life, death and resurrection, and its triumphant completion at his return in glory, is reflected in almost every line of the New Testament. Sometimes indeed it had unfortunate results, as when Christians in Thessalonika gave up work for good on the grounds that the Lord's return was very soon. St Paul had to urge them to fulfil their normal duties.

This reading of the New Testament poses problems, both theoretical and practical, for Christians today. Does it not undermine all that Christ taught? Further, if Jesus' ethical teaching is so closely linked to his idea of the kingdom, which he believed was breaking in through his ministry and would come in its fullness very soon, how can it apply to us? If someone gets up and announces that the world will come to its destined end in the year 2000 (as so many announced that it would in 1000 AD) and the bimillennium passes with everything unchanged, the other parts of the prophet's message are bound to be regarded as less than credible. Two points can be made in relation to this difficulty. First, any belief that human life finds its fulfilment in history, rather than in an eternal realm above history, is bound to have a degree of urgency about it. The Jews of the Old Testament believed that history had a beginning, a middle and an end. To teach people about that end, an end in the light of which everything else is to be judged, is inevitably to invest the message with a degree of urgency. Secondly, in one sense, Christ's prediction that the end was soon, was true, for he himself was raised from the dead and the first Christians saw this as the first fruit of the general resurrection. Raising of the dead was a sign of the end, a sign that the kingdom of God had come. So in a decisive sense the kingdom has come; though not yet in its fullness.

The crucial question as far as the ethical teaching of Jesus is concerned is how, in the light of this, does his teaching apply to us. The answer can be approached by considering a particular saying that is not related to resistance. Jesus taught, 'Give to him who begs from you, and do not refuse him who would borrow from you'.[2] Anyone who wants to take the teaching of Christ seriously must begin by asking what such a saying might mean. For example, who counts as those who 'beg from you'? Does this include buskers in the street and advertisements for charities in the newspaper? Secondly, we cannot avoid asking whether it would actually be morally right to give to everyone, despite what Christ said. It could hardly be in the best interests of an alcoholic to give him five pounds every time he asked you for it. Besides, there are many claims upon us, not simply that of the person who asks. The five pounds might morally belong to your children, or the starving. So, on many occasions we might have to conclude that it would be morally wrong to obey this command literally. So what function do this and similar injunctions of Jesus perform?

First, the saying opens us up to the need of the person who asks and forces us to take him and his request seriously. If we don't give, it has to be for good, moral reasons. This reverses the normal situation, in which we begrudge giving to people and harden our hearts to them. On the basis of the teaching of Jesus there is a *prima facie* case for meeting any request. The burden of proof is on the one who would refuse. Secondly, the saying acts as a standard of judgement. In facing it and the request of the one who asks, we find not only proper reasons for not acceding to the request, but also a begrudging attitude in our heart, a lack of generosity. Thirdly, the saying points us to a transformed reality in which life is lived on a very different basis. In the fullness of the kingdom, life is lived on the basis of mutual giving and receiving, and total inter-dependence. In the kingdom there are no barriers of pride which stop us making our needs known to others, or barriers of selfishness which stop us giving to the other person when they ask. So, fourthly, if we do decide to give supplicants what they ask for, it will not be for ordinary moral reasons. It will be an expression of the spirit of generosity which characterizes life in the kingdom and it will be a sign of that kingdom. In this life, good reasons for not acceding to someone's request can nearly always be found. Sometimes, despite those reasons, we want to give to them, and this saying enjoins us to do so. If we do so, it will not be simply 'for the good' of the other person, but as a sign of that new order in which the whole basis of life is transformed into one of total trust in God and one of openness, trust and hope towards others.

In the light of this general understanding of the sermon on the mount it is possible to look more closely at the three examples given in Matthew 5. 38–42. If insulted, these verses say to us, not only refrain from retaliation but be willing to bear further insults. If someone has done you a wrong, do not take legal action; instead, make a conscious act of generosity towards the person against whom you have a grievance. If someone forces you to do something, be willing to do even more than he asks. The purpose of this behaviour is not primarily to bring about a change of attitude in the other person. It is, first and foremost, an expression of trust in God. Instead of taking action ourselves to right a wrong or throw off an oppressor, we are to put our whole trust in the one whose supreme responsibility this is. Secondly, this act of trust, though made for its own sake, rests on the assumption that God is trustworthy and is indeed taking action to make justice prevail. Normally in this life wrongdoers are brought to court. It is right that this should be done, both as an act of justice and as part of the process of creating an ordered society within which alone human life can flourish. If we do not take the person to court the underlying moral assumption is that we are trusting God to vindicate the right, and that he is in the process of doing just that; he is at work ensuring that wrongdoers fall and the meek inherit the earth. He is bringing in the new order. Jesus acted on this assumption, with total trust, and taught others to do the same. It led to his death: but in his resurrection all that he had lived by and taught was validated. Many Christians feel called by God to walk the same path, trusting that God will likewise vindicate them, either in this life or in the life of the world to come. Other Christians, however, believe that though this may be a legitimate vocation for some, its adoption by the majority presupposes that certain fundamental changes will already have taken place in the way human beings and states behave.

The reason for this is that although in some decisive sense the kingdom of God has come on earth in the life, death and resurrection of Christ, yet it has not come in its fullness. Until it comes in its fullness, the wicked are still likely to prosper and the poor to be oppressed. The cry that goes up from so many psalms, the cry of the violated innocent one, a cry which Christ made his own, still goes up. 'How long O Lord?'[3] This means that, for as long as this life endures, Christians will be conscious not only of the claims of the kingdom of God, but also of the duties of civil society.

There are signs of this tension in the Gospels. First, Christ assumed the presence of the Torah. The Old Testament and the scribal interpretation which surrounded it were at the heart of the society which he addressed. Although he rejected much of the scribal interpretation he did not reject the Old Testament. Indeed, he said he had come to fulfil it. Much of the Old Testament is concerned with the moral, legal and practical procedures that are necessary for the existence of any human society. It is concerned with justice and the implementation of justice in a world of recalcitrant human beings. Secondly, Christ did not unequivocally call everyone to live out the ethic of the kingdom in a total way. He appears, for example, to have had both respect and affection for a number of centurions whom he left to follow their secular calling. He did not, as he did with the rich young ruler, tell the centurion to leave all and follow him. Similarly, although too much should not be read into John the Baptist's advice to soldiers, 'Rob no one by violence or by false accusation, and be content with your wages',[4] it does imply that for Luke there was no fundamental incompatibility between the Christian ethic and being a soldier. They were told to behave professionally as soldiers, not to give up soldiering altogether.

In every age the Christian Church has struggled to reconcile the ethical teaching of Jesus with the duties and responsibilities of everyday life. One famous way of resolving the problem has been to make a distinction between the counsels of perfection and the precepts of ordinary morality.

According to this view, there is a basic morality which is obligatory on all Christians. In addition, there is a way of life characterized by poverty, chastity and obedience, to which God may call particular people. At the Reformation Martin Luther rejected this double standard, one for monks and nuns and the other for ordinary Christians. However, he did not feel able to escape setting up a new dualism. According to Luther, God rules the world in two different ways. He rules by persuasive love in the hearts of true believers. He also rules by the sword all those who will not respond to love. As no Christian is perfect, this means that everyone lives in two kingdoms and is ruled by both love and the sword.

No Christian can or should feel entirely happy about any of these attempts to reconcile the teaching of the sermon on the mount with prudential considerations. Nor is it surprising that in every generation there should arise Christians who will have nothing to do with such attempts, and who believe that they are all forms of illegitimate compromise, refusals to take Christ at his word and obey him. For example, Sider and Taylor write:

> We do not believe God has a double ethic. We do not believe God ordains a higher ethic for especially devout folk and a lower ethic for the masses. We do not believe that God intends Christians to wait until the millennium to obey the Sermon on the Mount. We do not believe God commands one thing for the individual and another for that same person as a public official.[5]

Despite this strong statement, some form of dualism is inescapable for the Christian. This is because we live 'between the times'. In the Eucharist the congregation makes the acclamation 'Christ has died. Christ is risen. Christ will come again.' Christians live between the time of Christ's rising and the time of his coming again. It is true that in the past Christians have tried to collapse the tension to which this gives rise by misconceived forms of dualism. The effect has often been that justice has not been done to the claims of Jesus's teaching, and there has been a too easy compromise with the standards of the world. Some have tried to collapse the tension by accepting the standards of natural morality and ignoring the claims of the sermon on the mount. But others have suggested that we can live as though the kingdom had already come in its fullness. Both are wrong.

The ethical teaching of Jesus and its bearing on our lives now may be summed up in the following points. First, Jesus teaches the ethic of the kingdom of God. It is the ethic of an environment in which God rules without let or hindrance. The wicked have received their due desert and the righteous flourish. This is the setting in which the pure see God, the hungry are fed, the meek rule and those who mourn are comforted. Secondly, Jesus put this ethic before us and called us to live under God's rule. He called us to live by total trust in God and with an unconditioned love and forgiveness for others. It is an absolute ethic, in that it makes no concessions to the world we know. When two brothers who were quarrelling over an inheritance asked Jesus to settle the disp-ute he said, 'who made me a divider or judge over you? Beware of all covetousness.'[6] In the world as we have it there are innumerable disputes, and lawyers are essential to ensure that they are settled with the maximum fairness. Jesus put before people the vision of a world ruled by perfect love, a world without disputes or lawyers. Thirdly, before anything else, this absolute ethic judges us. It is the light which shows up what is going on in our own hearts. And it reveals the compromises made necessary by a sinful world, as the compromises they are. Fourthly, this ethic beckons us to obey it, so far as we can, taking into account the other moral claims upon us. Fifthly, there are some misconceived forms of dualism which must be rejected. The ethic of Jesus claims all Christians, not only those, like monks or nuns, who try to live out its injunctions literally. Again, the ethic of Jesus is concerned with our outward actions and not only with the disposition of our heart, though of course it was the latter which Jesus stressed. Not least, the ethic of Jesus bears on our role in the state as well as on our private lives. Sixthly, this ethic is not, however, the only claim upon us. Because of the dualism which is an inextricable part of the New Testament perspective, there is always a conflict between the absolute claims of the ethic of Jesus and the duties that impinge on us as citizens. For we are members of an earthly order held together, in part, by coercion, as well as members of the new order of Christ's society.

The import of this can be made clear by an example. How should society treat convicted criminals? The Gospels tell us that we should forgive people without limit, until seventy times seven. Should a criminal therefore simply be forgiven and released? This is what a Tolstoyan interpretation of the teaching of Jesus would advocate. It assumes we can act literally on the sayings of Jesus and allow them to override totally all other considerations. Should we, on the other hand, let strict justice take its course, and say that the teaching of Jesus is applicable to individual behaviour but not to the way a state should behave? This is what a Lutheran interpretation tends towards, though it does stress that when a criminal is punished it must be with a motive of love in the heart. But this is to collapse the proper tension by leaving the ethic of Jesus out of account, as far as the objective norms of state behaviour are concerned.

The position taken here is that considerations of justice have to be taken into account. The criminal cannot simply be released. Society has to be protected and the criminal himself, together with others who may be tempted to behave in a similar fashion, have to be deterred. The ethic of Jesus is, however, related to the judiciary and penal system in two ways. First of all it judges it. It reveals the hardened structures, and the hardened hearts that make them necessary, for what they are. These structures are concessions to human sin, ways of managing it. The judge and jailer, no less that the convicted criminal, stand before this tribunal. Secondly, the system is beckoned to approximate, so far as it can, to the ideal of perfect love. In other words, the good of the accused and the good of the person in prison are legitimate considerations. They are to be treated not simply as objects of an impersonal justice, but as children of God with love. Although the humanitarian approach concerned with the rehabilitation of the prisoner is not now officially advocated, it is based upon principles that are not only secular but deeply Christian; and this concern is not simply something for individual people of good-will. It is a way in which the ethic of Jesus bears upon the structures of the state.

What has been outlined in relation to the judiciary and penal system applies *mutatis mutandis* to other uses of state force. The role of the army in Northern Ireland, for example, is made necessary by human sinfulness (English as well as Irish). In the light of the sermon on the mount, it is shown up in all this tragic sinfulness. That same light bids us to work, not simply to contain violence, but also to love and reconcile. This may be a political necessity: more deeply, it is a Christian imperative.

The first chapter argued that an ethic of love does not rule out the use of force when that force is exercised by good-will towards the good of the criminal or aggressor. This chapter has suggested that the key texts in the sermon on the mount do not point unambiguously to the inadmissibility of all force. More fundamentally, the very difficult question of how we are to understand the ethical teaching of Jesus as a whole has been considered. It has been argued that because Christians live between Christ's rising and his coming again, there is an inescapable tension between the duties that arise out of our membership of civil society and the absolute ideal of Jesus which claims, judges and beckons us to approximate to it, so far as we can under the conditions of sinful human existence; and that it does this in relation to both our personal and official roles.

Before examining in details the pacifist and just war positions that can be drawn out of the argument so far presented, it is necessary to consider fundamental questions about man and society. For how we make up our mind on many issues depends in large measure upon basic presuppositions about what human beings are like.

Notes

1. Matthew 5.38–42.
2. Matthew 5.42.
3. Revelation 6.10.
4. Luke 3.14.
5. *Nuclear Holocaust and Christian Hope,* p.132.
6. Luke 12.14.

CHAPTER THREE

The world in which we live

History seems a succession of wars: the Hundred Years War, the Thirty Years War, wars against Spain and France, the English Civil War, the Napoleonic Wars and the two horrendous World Wars of this century — to mention just a fraction of the wars that have taken place in a small part of the globe. When we turn from the past to the present there is hardly a country in the world free of some form of civil strife or war. The history of the human race is a history of war.

What are the causes of this sad state of affairs? During this century, scientists have sought the cause in some aspect of our biological or psychological make-up. Comparisons have been made with animal behaviour, and it has been suggested that as birds will string out at equal distances along telegraph wires and animals will warn others off their patch of ground, so human beings are driven by a 'territorial imperative'. Other writers have posited a flaw in our genetic make-up; or have looked to the emergence of *homo sapiens* in evolution as a weapon-bearing rather than a tool-making animal, these weapons together with man's developing brain enabling him to triumph against other species. Psychologists have explored the possibility of an aggressive instinct deriving from psycho-social factors rather than genetic ones. Yet none of these theories has succeeded in winning the field against its rivals; and they all suffer from one fatal flaw. They fail to do justice to man as a spiritual being. When human beings war with one another, they do so not as advanced animals but as potential gods. It is this, as much as anything, which both forces us to see our wars, when we are fighting them, in the most exalted terms, and which can result in behaviour more destructive than that of any animal. People sometimes talk of 'behaving like an animal'. But which other animal would exterminate seven million of his kind by putting them in gas ovens? Which other animal systematically tortures his fellows?

Man is, in Disraeli's striking phrase, 'half ape, half angel'. But the angel is twisted, and the result is that we are both willing to die for a noble cause and, sometimes, to kill ruthlessly for an ignoble one.

Many people who live in Western liberal societies still profess to believe in the essential reasonableness and goodness of human beings. In practical terms this belief expresses itself in attempts to create humane educational, social and penal systems. If people are treated decently and properly educated, the thought runs, they will eventually respond. There is a rationality and goodness in them which has been hidden or warped by a defective upbringing and education. If that real self can be touched through kind treatment and enabled, through better education, to see things, differently, they will change. This is a noble vision, but it needs to take into account both the way we do in fact behave and the way we see ourselves in films, plays and novels. One of the best known literary challenges to the idea of the essential goodness of human beings has come from William Golding. In his novel, *The Inheritors,* he contrasted two tribes, one on the threshold of human consciousness and one just past it. The pre-human society is characterized by a sense of social unity, kindness and innocence. The society which had evolved into self-consciousness is marked by orgies, alcohol, violence and sacrifice to a cruel god. In *Lord of the Flies,* Golding set a bunch of cherubic faced choirboys in paradisal conditions. Within days they had split up into gangs and were fighting one another to the death. In Golding's world everything has gone wrong, even religion, perhaps especially religion. In *The Spire,* the dean of a cathedral builds a vast spire — to the glory of God. Yet, also, of course, to his own glory. The foundations are not adequate and it all comes crashing down. These fables express a much more sombre view of human nature than is often allowed. In a rare television interview, William Golding was asked how he had come to such a bleak vision. He said it was in the second World War, when he was in the Royal Navy. One night on board ship, he realized that the Nazis were not just outside, over the water, there was a Nazi in everyone.

Golding is not alone in his attempt to challenge Western liberal assumptions. Almost every novelist and playwright does so in one way or another. Another Nobel prize winner, Patrick White, in *The Riders in the Chariot* re-works the crucifixion of Christ in contemporary Australia. There are clear parallels not only with what happened in Palestine but also with what happened in Nazi Germany. Himmelfarb, a Jewish professor who has fled from Germany, is strung up by his mates in the factory where he works. Literary critics have been divided in their reaction to *The Riders in the Chariot*. Some have said that it is absurd to equate the petty spitefulness of Australian suburbia with the Nazi holocaust or the crucifixion of Christ. Others have argued, however, that, whatever form it takes, evil is one and its tendency the same.

From a Christian point of view such works are a necessary corrective to the notion that the ideal of love is the only contribution Christianity has to make to our understanding of human life. For Christianity is not only about our potential to love. It is no less about our failure to love. As Reinhold Niebuhr put it:

> Christianity is a religion which measures the total dimension of human existence not only in terms of the final norm of human conduct, which is expressed in the law of love, but also in terms of the fact of sin. It believes that, though Christ is the true norm of every man, every man is also in some sense a crucifier of Christ.[1]

Yet, though it is true, on a Christian perspective, that 'every man is also in some sense a crucifier of Christ' we have still to explore why this is so. Is it because we see what is evil and deliberately choose it for its own sake? Is it because we see clearly the good and decide consciously to spurn and scorn it? We cannot rule out the possibility of such behaviour, and it is certainly present in the story of Satan who, living in the immediate presence of God, chose consciously to rebel. It is also seen in the story of Faust as well as in a host of lesser tales. Nevertheless, such a picture seems an over-dramatic explanation for most human behaviour. How many people are motivated by a desire to do evil? How often have we deliberately defied God in full consciousness of what we are doing? Graham Greene tells the story of a Dominican priest he knew who confided to a friend that, in all his time of hearing confessions, he had never come across a 'mortal' sin, that is, one committed in deliberate defiance of God. So how do we account for the fact that human beings killed the Son of God, and that daily the most terrible atrocities are committed?

There is no single cause, for we are all characterized by different forms of blindness, weakness and wrongdoing. There is, shared by us all, a basic failure of the imagination. We do not take in the reality of other people or the hurt that they are experiencing. If we experienced their reality in the same way as we do our own, their pain as ours, it would be very different. But they impinge on our consciousness as through a mist. There is also, shared by all, a natural weakness, so that we find it difficult to place anything before our own comfort, or security. In particular, we find it difficult to stand out against the disapproval of others. Yet all these forms of negligence, weakness and deliberate wrong-doing hardly seem adequate to account for the mountain of suffering which human beings have inflicted on one another; nor does it account for the fact that even in the most shocking atrocities there is some twisted good in things evil. For the horrifying fact is that some of the most terrible deeds have been committed in the name of good. So we are forced back again to a consideration of our essentially spiritual being. We are not just animals, even morally conscious animals, but beings haunted by a sense of the absolute. This expresses itself in a desire to live for, and even die for, something greater than ourselves. We seek causes with which to identify. Sometimes it is the justifiable grievance of an oppressed nation or class: sometimes it is a political ideal, like the liberty espoused by followers of 'the good old cause' of Cromwell's men. Sometimes it is a religious belief, or interpretation of religious belief. As with everything human there are a variety of factors at work when we are taken up by some cause. Sometimes it is a way of forgetting or sublimating the frustrations and discontents of personal or family life. Sometimes it is a way of giving significance to an insignificant personal existence through the success of a football team or a victory in war. Often, however, the cause leads us truly to give of ourselves. We give time, energy, perhaps even our life to it. That is why patriotism, but not only patriotism, is an ethical paradox. It expresses both altruism and egoism. Yet the dilemma goes even beyond this, for in finding meaning and significance for our lives through the causes we serve, we have a tendency to absolutize them: and, behind this, lurks a fundamentally spiritual problem, a failure to accept our creaturely status and a tendency to adopt a god-like view. It is true that in some periods of history, notably the eighteenth century, wars have been limited to small groups of professionals pitted against one another in relatively confined areas. It is also the case that some thinkers, notably Clausewitz, have looked at war in rational terms as a legitimate instrument of policy. But it is part of the problem of war, perhaps the problem, that because of our spiritual status, albeit warped, we are not, in the twentieth century, able either to conceive or practise war in that kind of way.

Each one of us is the product of a particular history and culture. We occupy a particular point in time and space. We are conditioned, limited and finite. Yet we have infinite longings. We have a capacity to apprehend the unconditioned, the unlimited, the infinite, as it touches our souls through the claims and grace of our circumstances. Yet, instead of accepting the partial perspective of our status and acknowledging an absolute beyond anything we can fully grasp, we tend to absolutize our own point of view. This gives a spurious reassurance, blinding us to the partial, limited nature of our view, and distorting the touch of the eternal upon us by treating something finite as if it were infinite.

Our plight is even worse than this, however, for not only do we absolutize our own point of view but we seek to impose it on others. By dominating others, ideologically, religiously, or politically, we reinforce our blindness to our vulnerable, mortal status, and further poison our relationship to the absolute by keeping our ego at the centre not only of our own life but those of others as well. As Niebuhr has put it:

Man is the only finite creature who knows that he is
finite and he is therefore tempted to protest against his
fate. One form which this protest takes is his imperialistic ambition, his effort to overcome his insignifi-
cance by subordinating other life to his individual or
collective will.[2]

So it is that the will-to-live becomes transmuted into the
will-to-power and the will-to-power hides itself under a cloak
of universal values. So Niebuhr again:

Caesars and saints are made possible by the same
structure of human character. Human progress is
possible only because some human spirits will on
occasion transcend the presuppositions of their society
and envisage more perfect goals for life than their
society has been able to comprehend. This very capacity
will always make it possible for imperial individuals and
groups to arise and seek to subordinate life to their will
and purpose. Upon it all utopian dreams of perfect
harmony will be shattered.[3]

We live in a world with radical differences of perspective.
Those brought up on a Kibbutz find it both natural and right
to fight in the Israeli army. Those brought up in a Palestinian
refugee camp, nurtured on stories of how grandfather was
forced to flee from the ancestral olive groves around Tel
Aviv, have a natural sympathy for the PLO. Similarly in
Northern Ireland, history, culture and religion have formed
two communities that are deeply antagonistic to one another.
What makes such conflicts so difficult to resolve and their
violence so bitter? It is not simply a failure of imagination, a
failure to see that those on the other side are human beings
with fellow feelings. It is not simply lack of courage to stand
out against the tribe. It is that each cause has some legitimate
right and this right becomes absolutized. The cause becomes
something to live for and die for. Governments that go to war
think of this not simply as a rational activity, a venture in
which they stand to gain more than they will lose, but a cause
in which right is on their side. This was true even of Nazi

Germany. There were many grievances, as a result of the Versailles settlement, on which Hitler could and did build. Goebbels in his diary wrote of 'that great gangster Churchill', and imagines Germans in a hundred years' time looking back at the heroic German people struggling against disaster. He worked with the image of himself as a moral hero. A whole people were deceived. But before they were deceived, those who deceived them had deceived themselves. They had convinced themselves that what they were doing was in the name of some great good.

Differences in perspective are inherent in our finite existence. These differences carry with them clashes of interest. These clashes are not just misunderstandings that can be resolved by talking the matter through. As one prince said to another in sixteenth century Italy: 'We understand one another very well. We both want Italy.' Nor can these clashes of interest be resolved simply on rational grounds. For human beings are spiritual beings, with a propensity to give themselves totally to that which is greater than themselves. Tragically, what happens is that human beings give themselves totally to some human cause, their country, their religion, an ideology, or a political idea, that they invest with absolute authority. Does this tendency point to an inescapable relativism? It seems we should resist dying for, let alone killing for, any cause at all. This question is considered in Chapter Five. But first it is necessary to consider another inescapable feature of human existence, our organization into states.

With the world divided into great power blocs, it is highly tempting to think that if only the ordinary people of the world could reach out to one another across national and idealogical boundaries, the threat of war would melt. The technical name for this point of view is anarchism. Anarchy has become a smear word because it has been, and is, so often associated with violence. But the essence of anarchy is a belief that government is the root of all evil. Not all anarchists have been violent; some have been pacifists and some have been radical Christian idealists. Anarchy is an idea worth taking seriously, if only to see how sadly wrong it is. For Christians, ever since they began to reflect seriously on these matters, have concluded that government, however much we might chaff under it, is necessary. Thomas Aquinas stressed that government is natural to man. Because we are essentially social beings, it is natural for us to come together in a co-operative endeavour; and it is natural that there should be some political centre to reconcile and harmonize our different interests. Martin Luther, by contrast, emphasized the unnaturalness of government, in that it is only because we are sinful that we need it; but he had no doubt that we did need it. In the Garden of Eden, God ruled the world by the moving of one finger. But because Adam sinned and mankind is fallen, sin would know no bounds unless the state limited the amount of harm we can do to one another. Human beings are wild animals who, given the chance, would tear one another apart. The state acts as a cage to keep us from devouring our fellow beings. So government is a result of the fall, in that the fall has made it necessary. It is also a partial remedy for the fall, in that it keeps sin within certain bounds.

If Aquinas's view is taken to express the role of consent in government and Luther's is taken to express the role of coercion, the two views can be seen to be complementary. Government depends on a mixture of consent and coercion. It is not, as Mao suggested in his famous line, that power **grows** out of the barrel of a gun, simply a matter of coercion. As Hannah Arendt argued,[4] some consent is necessary, even if only the consent of those who hold the guns for you. Yet nor, on the other hand, does a country hold together on the basis of consent alone. Who, if it was entirely voluntary, would pay their income tax?

So human beings need government. We need it because it is natural for us to come together under one authority; we need it because, unless there is an authority with the power to coerce, we would not hold together as a society at all. But do we need the present system of nation states? Particularly during this century men have longed for some world authority that could resolve the chaos of our international anarchy. But a sad fact has to be faced. Although we have the potential for such authority in the United Nations, that authority as at present constituted has no power to enforce its decisions. It can attempt to persuade, as also do the various international courts. But, until it is constituted differently and has the power to impose its will on member states, those states will continue to go their own way when they think the matter is one that concerns their vital interests.

There is also the further, more troubling question, as to whether if we did have a world government it would be other than the biggest empire the world has known. What checks and balances would there be? What would prevent it being a tyranny writ very large? However, at the moment and for the foreseeable future, we live in different states, and this is an inescapable part of our condition. It is tempting to think of the people of the Soviet Union or the United States or Iran, as though they could be isolated from the government or ideology that we may so much dislike. But though we can make such a separation in theory, in practice the people of the United States, the Soviet Union and Iran and every other country in the world, actually need a government of some kind and we have to deal with the government they have. There is a further terrible paradox. If a war breaks out, it is above all the government of the enemy that has to be preserved, for governments alone have the power to negotiate an end to hostilities. The one exception might be if there is an alternative government ready and able to take over. Our natural tendency is to blame the government of the enemy and to want to cripple them rather than their people, who for the most part will have been led unwittingly into the conflict. Yet, for the sake of those people, for the possibility of bringing the war to an end at all, it will usually be essential not to totally incapacitate the organs of government. The atomic bomb could easily have been dropped on the Japanese government and high command. But who then would have sued for peace?

As human beings we live under governments. These governments are in power to safeguard the interests of the people over whom they are set. The concept of self-interest is a perfectly proper one, both inevitable and right, for nations. It is horribly true that nations too often conceive of their interests wrongly or only from a short term point of view. But it is perfectly proper for them to think in terms of interest, as it is for any organized human grouping. An individual human can sacrifice his or her interests out of love for another. A father can dive into the sea to rescue his child, even at risk of his own life. It is not open to institutions to make such gestures. The headmaster of a school, for example, is not at liberty to give away all the school science equipment to a needier establishment. He has been given a position of trust to build up the educational work of that particular school. Similarly, members of a government, whether that government has been elected or not, have a particular responsibility to safeguard and further the interests of their people.

The coinage of relationships between states is power. Power, in its most general sense, means the ability to achieve a chosen goal. In this sense power is an essential aspect of any being. A powerless being is a non-existent being. God has all the power that belongs to him as God. We have the power that belongs to us as human beings, for example, power to manipulate nature to our use. But power can be exercised in various ways, notoriously by persuasion or coercion; and there are many forms of coercion, most notably economic or military. In relationships between individuals the power factor can be equalized and the element of coercion transcended. Friends try to relate to one another without any form of domination or threat. But in relationships between organized groupings the power factor is always present and usually of paramount importance. In relationships between capital and labour, between government and the trade unions, and between states, the ability to achieve a chosen goal, whether or not the other party consents to it, is crucial. This is not to suggest that all relationships between states simply reflect their relative power; that would be a crude determinism. It is to suggest that in considering the properly moral goals of a state, its power in relation to other states will, as a matter of brute fact, be a crucial factor in deciding whether and how those goals are attainable.

There is one more feature of the way states behave that cannot be avoided, their tendency to expand their territory if they are able to do so. Although it is possible to point to states which do not now seem to exhibit this tendency, this may simply reflect their present relative weakness. For example, the Netherlands, Belgium and Sweden have in the past all controlled empires. This tendency to expand is not always, or even most usually, simply for aggrandisement. All states have a defensive/aggressive mentality which makes them strive for more and more secure borders. A good modern example is Israel, which both feels threatened by and threatens its neighbours; though in the case of Israel there is a complicating fact in that, in the declaration of independence, her borders were not defined and have not been defined since. A state without borders is tempted to expand to protect those on the periphery, but this creates a new periphery. Another example of the tendency to expand is the Soviet Union's policy of buffer states. No state ever feels entirely secure, so it can always discover measures it ought to take in the interest of its safety. Because it is liable to overestimate the external threat and underestimate the extent to which its own imperialistic ambitions are clothed in defensive rhetoric, the measures it takes will themselves be seen as threatening to others.

A great deal can and should be done to understand the history, culture and outlook of an opposite ideology or country. Indeed it would seem the first requirement of Christian love to try to enter imaginatively and sympathetically into the viewpoint of those who are posited as enemies. For example, it is possible to enter with much more understanding than is usually shown into that much derided group, the Afrikaners. A novel like *The Covenant* by James Michener imparts a sense of their struggle, not least against the British who invented the concentration camp to deal with them; of their ideals and sense of destiny. Yet, in the end, when every effort has been made to understand and we can feel something of the moral strength and appeal of their point of view, we still have to make a moral choice between their policies and the aspirations of the majority in South Africa. Whatever the strength of their case, whatever the hypocrisy of the white liberal, a choice still has to be made between eternal white supremacy (however disguised) and a more representative system. Similarly, much can be done to enter into the Soviet perspective. We can understand something of the legacy that the Tartar yoke left on Russia, a tradition of secrecy and autocracy which, without a European

Reformation or Renaissance, were left essentially unchallenged. We can understand how a vast country with no natural borders leads to a policy which requires a large standing army and a comforting surround of buffer states. Similarly the history of this century, which saw the new Marxist-Leninist regime continually invaded or interfered with and over twenty million dead in World War 2, goes some way to explaining the existence of large conventional forces deployed for a blitzkreig policy; a deployment which, so the rulers hope, will ensure that any future war will be won quickly, and off their own soil. An understanding of this can do much to dispel unnecessary suspicion and paranoia. Nevertheless, hard choices still have to be made about a system which still retains a missionary zeal and which, like every empire in history, is inclined to inch its way outward if it can do so without inordinate cost.

Western liberals, particularly those of a Christian persuasion, are prone to construct a world in their own image, a world of amenable people and accommodating systems. But the world also contains hard men and uncompromising systems. Marxist-Leninism is a system with a long-term goal, which has certainly not been abandoned, however much the means to achieve it may have changed. Islam, similarly, is a political system, as well as a religion, every bit as determined as Marxist-Leninism, and one which may in the long run be its most formidable rival. Christians within the western liberal system face a double dilemma. On the one hand they have to force themselves to face the fact that the world contains both ruthless men and ruthless systems. On the other hand, if it is judged that these must not be allowed to encroach, opposition has to be mounted with a sense of shared finitude and fallibility. The crusade mentality is sure it is fighting the cause of the just against the unjust; in religious terms, the cause of God against his enemies. Yet, as was suggested earlier in the chapter, it is just this attitude which makes human conflict so intractable, bitter and destructive. It is just this attitude, in which one's own cause is absolutized, that a Christian will want to resist; for such an attitude is an attempt to step out of our creaturely status. Whatever the difficulties, moral choices have to be made; but they have to be made and stood up for, with an awareness that both the choice and the resulting action, is flawed, frail and fallible.

The world in which we live is one in which, ineluctably, we are part of some organized political system; at the present stage of history this is, for most of us, the nation-state. These states, like all organized human groupings try to safeguard their own interests and they are right to do so in so far as this can be done without impinging on the interests of others. Nor is there any escape from the crucial role played by power in the relation of one state to another as each seeks to protect its essential interests. We, who are members of these political systems, are moral beings, who, despite our flawed natures, are under obligation to discriminate between the more and less corrupt. Furthermore, we are also essentially spiritual beings, haunted by the absolute and likely therefore to invest our own judgements with a sense of absolute rightness; a temptation which must be resisted at the same time as we resist the alternative, which is to make no attempt to discriminate at all, throwing up our hands with a sense of the relativity of all things.

These considerations, together with the other features of human life explored earlier in the chapter, the differences of perspective that will always be present and the way we invest these differences with absolute significance, make conflict inevitable. Conflict is not an entirely bad thing. Indeed, as has been said, 'conflict is liberty'. The alternatives of totalitarianism and imperialism are usually, and rightly, rejected. But, in rejecting them, we are opting for a world in which conflict of one kind or another (not always armed conflict) is endemic. It is within this world, not a fairytale world, that we have to think about the ethics of resistance and non-resistance.

Notes

1. Reinhold Niebuhr, *Christianity and Power Politics,* Scribner's, NY, 1940, p.2.
2. Reinhold Niebuhr p.156.
3. Reinhold Niebuhr p.158.
4. Hannah Arendt, *On Violence,* Allen Lane, 1969.

CHAPTER FOUR

Resistance and pacifism

It used to be believed, even by Reinhold Niebuhr, that Jesus taught a doctrine of non-resistance. This was partly due to the Authorised Version translation of Matthew 5.39, 'But I say unto you, that ye resist not evil'. (The RSV also uses the word resist. 'But I say to you, do not resist one who is evil'.) Yet it is clear from the Gospels that in some crucial sense Jesus himself *did* resist all evil. He cast out devils, he healed the sick, he denounced hypocrisy, he prayed that God's kingdom might come on earth. Indeed, as St Augustine pointed out a long time ago, when Jesus was struck on the cheek at his trial, instead of accepting it silently or turning the other cheek, he answered back. 'If I have spoken wrongly, bear witness to the wrong; but if I have spoken rightly, why do you strike me?' (John 18.23)[1]

During this century, partly as a result of the impact of psychoanalysis, there has been a fresh realization of the importance of people standing up for themselves. From a psychological point of view, it is unhealthy for a person to allow others to treat them as a door mat. William Blake knew this, and in our own time D. H. Lawrence wrestled, both in his poetry and his prose, with distortions of Christian teaching that implied that we should allow others to walk over us. Blake and Lawrence taught both that it was psychologically wrong, for our feelings of resentment are still there, and also a denial of our proper human dignity. In *The Rainbow,* Ursula Brangwen tries to relate her Sunday world to her weekday world.

'Sell all thou hast, and give to the poor,' she heard on Sunday morning. That was plain enough, plain enough for Monday morning too. As she went down the hill to the station, going to school, she took the saying with her. 'Sell all thou hast, and give to the poor.' Did she want to do that? Did she want to sell her pearl-backed brush and mirror, her silver candlestick, her pendant, her lovely little necklace, and go dressed in drab like the Wherrys: the unlovely uncombed Wherrys, who were the 'poor' to her? She did not.

She walked this Monday morning on the verge of misery. For she *did* want to do what was right. And she *didn't* want to do what the gospels said. She didn't want to be poor — really poor. The thought was a horror to her: to live like the Wherrys, so ugly, to be at the mercy of everybody. 'Sell that thou hast, and give to the poor.' One could not do it in real life. How dreary and hopeless it made her!

Nor could one turn the other cheek. Theresa slapped Ursula on the face. Ursula, in a mood of Christian humility, silently presented the other side of her face. Which Theresa, in exasperation at the challenge, also hit. Whereupon Ursula, with boiling heart, went meekly away.

But anger, and deep, writhing shame tortured her, so she was not easy till she had again quarrelled with Theresa and had almost shaken her sister's head off.

'That'll teach you,' she said grimly. And she went away, unchristian but clean.

There was something unclean and degrading, about this humble side of Christianity. Ursula suddenly revolted to the other extreme.[2]

Even more important, from a moral point of view, could it ever be right to adopt a policy of total non-resistance to perceived evil? Ulrich Simon, who writes out of the experiences of having lost his parents in Auschwitz and his brother in a Soviet labour camp, has written:

Submission to evil powers as a policy seems to me so immoral that I had rather give up my Christian faith than subscribe to it.[3]

For these and other reasons, most pacifists today deny that Jesus taught non-resistance. This is helped by the NEB

translation of Matthew 5.39 'Do not *set yourself*
(μὴ ἀντιστῆναι) against the man who wrongs you'. Here the
emphasis is not on lack of resistance but on eschewing active
hostility. The phrase 'non-resistance' may once have had a
clear meaning, namely a denial of physical or armed
resistance; but, because it has come to be interpreted as a
rejection of resistance by any means at all, the phrase is best
dropped. This point is an important unifying factor, for
whatever else pacifists and non-pacifists might disagree
about, on this at least they can agree: Christians are called to
resist evil in all its forms. This goes way beyond mere verbal
agreement. For, deterrence depends first and foremost on the
will to resist. It also depends, of course, on effective means
with which to resist; but these are useless unless there lies
behind them a determination not to be overcome. General
Wolf Von Baudausin, who was with the German forces when
they invaded France, has said that the French had adequate
equipment and men with which to resist. What they lacked
was the will to do so. The Argentinian invasion of the
Falklands took place because the British, through a stupid
series of political blunders, conveyed to the Argentinians the
idea that an invasion of the Islands would not meet any
opposition. It was a classic failure of deterrence; and it was a
failure not only to have the right armoury in place at the right
time but a failure to convey the message that we had the will
to resist. The Falklands war, like all wars, was sad and tragic,
but it did have the result of indicating to the world that we
were still willing to use armed force to defend our citizens. In
the light of history it may be judged that more crucial than the
islands or even the lives of the islanders was the pulse of
determination our action sent through the whole NATO
deterrence posture.

Although this point has been made in relation to deterrence, it is no less true for forms of non-violent resistance.
The Swedish diplomat Raoul Wallenberg was stationed in
Budapest when it was occupied by the Nazis, and Jews were
being deported to the gas chambers. He managed to save
thousands of Jews by a combination of determination,
intelligence and bravado. What was crucial was his resolute
will to resist the evil.

Pacifists and non-pacifists unite to affirm the overriding importance of resisting evil. The disagreement comes in the means which it is morally legitimate to use in so resisting. A great deal has been written in the last fifty years about 'non-violent resistance'. Like 'non-resistance' this is a misleading phrase. It is misleading because many forms of resistance that claim to be non-violent are violent in one sense: they cause other people to suffer. Boycotts and strikes are forms of indirect coercion which can inflict quite severe degrees of hardship on others, as the boycott of Manchester cotton by Gandhi's followers caused the children of Lancashire to suffer. There is an important moral distinction to be made but it is not between violence and non-violence. It is between the direct use of force or coercion and indirect coercion. There is a difference between bombing a city and starving it into submission. But the latter course, in which hundreds might die of starvation, is also a form of coercion, albeit indirect.

Sider and Taylor make a distinction between what they call 'non-violent coercion' and 'lethal violence'. But this distinction blurs the real issue. Consider three conditional sentences in all of which coercion is present:

1. If you don't stop bullying your sister, you will go to your room.
2. If you don't stop bullying your sister, I will shoot you.
3. If you don't drop your gun, I'll shoot you (said to a bank-robber caught in the act).

On Sider and Taylor's analysis the crucial distinction is between the first statement and the other two, for these two both involve a weapon and therefore, in their terminology, are forms of 'lethal violence'. Yet, to many of us, the crucial distinction is rather between the second statement and the other two. For the coercion in the second statement is totally disproportionate. In the first and third statement it is strictly proportionate. If a man is holding up a bank and the police burst in and tell him to drop his gun, their action is the appropriate and proportionate response to the threat posed. It is the minimum use of coercion necessary to achieve a legitimate goal. In that sense it exactly corresponds to the parental statement to the child, that if he does not stop bullying his sister he will go to his room.

Clarity demands that distinctions be made between:

1. Total non-resistance (which both pacifists and non-pacifists reject).
2. Non-coercive resistance: that is, resistance that relies only on prayer and verbal persuasion.
3. Resistance that uses force or the threat of force.
4. Resistance that uses indirect coercion, through such means as strikes and boycotts.

These distinctions are necessary not only from the point of view of clarity but in order to dispel false notions of moral superiority. As a result of the influence of Gandhi and Martin Luther King most modern pacifism is a mixture of 2 and 4. Pacifists use both non-coercive resistance and certain forms of indirect coercion. There is nothing wrong with this. What is illegitimate however, is to use techniques of indirect coercion whilst claiming for them the moral aura that goes with non-coercive resistance.

Pacifism is an exceedingly varied phenomenon. It was only with the impact of the first World War, the crisis of the League of Nations from 1931-5, and the threat of Hitler and the introduction of conscription that the meaning of pacifism in Britain became clearly defined for the first time. These events forced pacifists to distinguish themselves from pacificist, those men who were doing everything possible to prevent war but who were in the end prepared to fight the Nazis.[4] Even so, there are many forms of pacifism. Yoder has distinguished at least twenty-five.[5]

All forms of Christian pacifism claim to be rooted in the New Testament and in particular to be based upon the teaching and example of Jesus. As was argued in Chapter Two, the evidence is rather against the view that Jesus taught pacifism *per se:* nevertheless, there is a strand within the New Testament upon which a Christian pacifism can be built. Secondly, Christian pacifists look to the history of the early

Church. But, here again, the evidence is not nearly so unambiguous as some pacifists have claimed. Certainly Christians were reluctant to join the Roman army until the conversion of Constantine in the fourth century, though the first evidence of Christians actually joining dates from AD 173 when a number were recruited by Marcus Aurelius near the Danube. But, were Christians reluctant because it was compulsory, at any rate above a certain rank, to sacrifice to Caesar, so that joining the army would have led them into idolatry? Or, because they believed, like Tertullian, that 'in disarming Peter, the Lord unbelted every soldier'? Again, did they, like Origen accept the necessity of force in general, but believe that Christians formed a special army of piety, upholding the work of the empire by their prayers?

In nearly all modern forms of Christian pacifism, two important elements can be distinguished. First, the element of witness to a different, higher order; a better world no longer dependent on any form of coercion. Secondly, the claim that a pacifist approach can achieve results in the world, that it is effective in bringing about peace with justice. Some pacifists, like Sydney Bailey, qualify this claim by saying that it is a long-term consequence of the witness to a better way. It is this latter element that has come to the fore during the last fifty years and which needs to be examined with particular care. First, the combination of non-coercive resistance and certain forms of indirect coercion is clearly effective in certain situations. It worked for Gandhi and it worked for Martin Luther King. Nevertheless, there were special features in both situations which would not always be present. Gandhi was a holy man in a country which greatly valued holy men. He was dealing with an enemy that was to some extent susceptible to moral considerations. Moreover, there were many in Britain who believed both on moral and practical grounds that the sooner Britain divested itself of its empire the better. Similarly, in the southern states of America, Martin Luther King could appeal to a Christian conscience, however dull or blinded it might have become. How would Stalin have reacted if confronted with Gandhi in the Soviet Union? There is enough evidence from the 28 million who perished in the great purges in the 1930s and in the way dissidents are treated today, to know that Gandhi's movement would have been strangled at birth. The same is even more true about Nazi Germany. A leader who did not scruple to exterminate 7 million Jews would hardly have spared much sympathy for an unarmed protestor. Indeed, as Hitler said to Lord Halifax, the British Foreign Secretary in 1937, 'All you have to do is shoot Gandhi: if necessary shoot some more congress leaders. You will be surprised how quickly the trouble will die down.'[6]

Non-coercive resistance coupled with forms of resistance using indirect coercion can be highly effective in certain circumstances. But not all. In many contexts these techniques would be useless: against ruthless foes with no more conscience than a psychopath they would be of no avail. Nevertheless, the Christian pacifist rightly brings into the picture some specifically Christian considerations: the power of the Holy Spirit, the providence of God and the resurrection hope. The Christian faith is based not only on the crucifixion but on the resurrection. It is not a cult of failure, but an affirmation of God's ultimate triumph. All this needs to be proclaimed. But can it be made the basis of a programme of political action? No. For although God's love, validated in the death and resurrection of Christ, will triumph, we are not a position to say when or how. Indeed Christ said: 'But of that day or that hour no one knows, not even the angels in heaven, nor the Son, but only the Father'.[7] What is called for is trust and hope in God. We do not have a programme giving the likelihood of success at a particular time. It must therefore be concluded that Christian pacifism is primarily an individual vocation, not a policy for government. For governments must make rational calculations and assess the steps that are most likely, in the foreseeable future, to safeguard the nation. Christian pacifism by contrast, is essentially a vocation to martyrdom. It consciously accepts the risk of rejection and earthly defeat. It goes the way of the Cross. The crucial point about martyrdom is that it has to be chosen under God by each individual for themselves. It cannot be imposed by others. It is open to individual Christians to walk this path if they conceive this as God's way for them. It is also open to a particular Church to do so. When the Anglican Church in

Iran was under great pressure in the early days after Ayatollah Khomeini's revolution, and its members being killed, including those of the Bishop's own family, there were those who saw this as the Church going the way of the cross and thereby witnessing to Christ. But can a nation become a martyr nation? No doubt there are circumstances in which a nation has no alternative but to submit and do what it can to retain some freedom in its subjugated state, as in Poland or other eastern European countries today. This is very different, however, from the situation that pertains when a nation has a chance of resisting. How could a Minister of Defence, charged with responsibility for the security of his country, allow affairs to deteriorate to the point when submission was the only option open? It is his clear duty to avoid getting anywhere near that impasse. Furthermore, whatever he might feel himself, as an individual Christian with a hope in God's ultimate triumph, how could he ask a whole nation to submit, when many, perhaps the majority, do not share such a faith or hope?

The importance of the distinction between what is open to the Church and what is closed to the nation can be seen in Augustine's and Luther's attitude to private self-defence. Although with Aquinas the Church began to teach the right of self-defence as such, whether by the state or an individual, this represented a change. Augustine did not allow it and Luther tried to make a further distinction. Luther said that if he was attacked when he was going about preaching the gospel, he would not defend himself. It would not be right for the work of the gospel to be defended by force of arms. On the other hand, he did admit the possibility that, if he was attacked *qua* citizen, it might be right for him to resist, in which case he would be acting with something akin to the power of citizen's arrest, not in his personal capacity but as a representative of the state. All Christians are members of the body politic, and so sharers in both the duties and the benefits of the state. It might therefore be right for the Church to claim for its members the ordinary protection most modern states afford to all their citizens, an appeal which the Anglican Church did in fact make in Iran. As loyal citizens, Christians, like others, are entitled to the protection of the state.

However, Luther was perhaps correct in suggesting that the Church, *qua* Church, should not be protected by force of arms. As was indicated in earlier chapters and as will be explored further later, the prime justification of the use of force is to provide the indispensible minimum conditions of a just order, both within a particular society and in the states system as a whole, without which there can be no human society. Christians, *qua* Christians, do not need this protection and should not claim it, even though a particular state may as a matter of principle, for its own stability, afford a degree of protection to the practise of a variety of religions. G.H.C. Macgregor has written:

> Christian pacifists have often been warned by self-styled 'realists' that we shall never bring in the Kingdom of God by acting in an evil world as if it were already here. Yet this is, I suggest, exactly what Jesus *did* teach: if only men were prepared to take God at his word and to order their lives here and now by the laws of a transcendent Kingdom, then the power of God would answer the cry of faith, and the Kingdom would break in upon them unawares.[8]

This is well said, but the implications of that stance have to be equally clearly stated. It is in an evil world that we will so act. This means that there is no guarantee of success in the short term, indeed the likelihood of failure, on the grounds that a disciple is not above his master. Such failure can be risked by the individual Christian and perhaps even by the Church in a particular locality. It is not a risk that can be taken by a government on behalf of their people as a whole.   —

Christian pacifism must be seen primarily as an individual vocation, akin to the vows of poverty, chastity and obedience taken by monks and nuns. In taking these vows they seek to witness to the possibility of a life lived totally for God and in trust upon him alone. It is obvious that, if everyone took these particular vows, human life as we know it would cease. But it is healthy that some should seek to live in this way, thereby witnessing to the possibility of Jesus's 'impossible possibility'. This does not mean that there is one standard for self-righteous, first class Christians, and a lower one for others who can be complacently content with the minimum. Against such a division the reformers rightly reacted. For the absolute ideal impinges upon us all, lawyer as well as monk, statesman as well as private citizen. As was suggested in Chapter Two, the norm of Jesus judges us and beckons us to approximate to it so far as we can, whilst taking into account the structures of civic life made necessary by our sinful state.

Macgregor argued that we should act now, in an evil world, as if the kingdom of God were already here. This is to collapse the tension between Christ's rising and his coming again by ignoring one half of the acclamation. It is open to a Christian to do this, as Christ himself did: but as a witness to a new order of things, not as a political strategy.

In the past, some forms of uncompromisingly Christian pacifism faced this difficulty frankly and withdrew, so far as they could, from the structures of civil society. In Canada and the United States today there are large tracts of farmland owned by members of the Amish community, a branch of the Mennonites. Many of these have little contact with the outside world, no telephones, or cars, and certainly none with military or state service of any kind. Some of the most challenging new style pacifism does not wish to follow that particular Mennonite path. Yoder, for example, in what he calls the pacifism of the Messianic community, argues that Christ's uncompromising demands are directed to all men. To be sure they cannot be obeyed until Jesus is acknowledged as Lord and his Spirit fills their lives: but Jesus, his demands and his Spirit, are for all, not just a withdrawn cultic minority. Thus, followers of this way will stay within public life as a witness. They can certainly be a witness. But can they at the same time legitimately accept public office? For public office means an intimate involvement in the structures of the state, including its coercive structures. Moreover government works on the basis of a prudent calculation of what is in the interest of the community as a whole. This will certainly include a concern for the defence of the community and a rational calculation of the steps that must be taken to ensure this. This does not preclude, in a British context, a person standing for Parliament on an avowedly pacifist platform, and trying over the course of time to achieve a majority and form a government of that persuasion. It does preclude a pacifist becoming a member of a government based on non-pacifist principles, as are all present governments.

Pacifism and non-pacifism belong together in the Church. This is not simply a matter of historical accident or tolerance — both views now being found, they should be allowed to exist together. The relationship between pacifism and non-pacifism is essential rather than accidental. They belong together as representing the twin poles of Christ's rising and his coming again. Together they witness to the tension that must continue to exist until his kingdom come.

Christian pacifism is to be seen primarily as a witness to a new order of reality, one totally transparent to the good, in which the defenceless are protected by God himself and in which the poor and oppressed are exalted. God, in his mercy, will assuredly bring forth from such witness many fruits, not only in the world to come but also in this world. Only it is of the very nature of genuine faith that we do not know in what form these fruits will come or when they will ripen. Those responsible for the safety of a community have to plan on the basis of reasonable calculation. They cannot take more risks than they think are justified, even in faith, with other people's lives, not least because very many of those for whom they are responsible will not have any religious convictions. A government has to act on the basis of careful assessment in the light of agreed realities. Those Christians who are not specially called by God to a pacifist witness will, as citizens, share something of the burden and duty of government as it exercises coercive power for the maintenance of that *pax-ordo-iustitia* without which no human society can survive.

This chapter has considered the claims of a complete Christian pacifism. Today, however, there are more Christians who count themselves nuclear pacifists than pacifists of this 'pure' type. The phrase 'nuclear pacifism' has come to mean different things to different people but it is best used to describe the view of those who are prepared to use force to resist aggression — up to a point: the point beyond which they will not go is the possession and use of nuclear weapons. But is nuclear pacifism *essentially* different from pacifism *tout simple?* The possession of nuclear weapons for deterrence purposes poses complex questions which are considered in later chapters, but the question must at least be raised here whether nuclear pacifism is different *in principle* from pacifism. Nuclear pacifism of course assumes that it is. But is it? Christian pacifism draws the line at resistance which would lead to the death or permanent injury of the person resisted. This means that, where there is a risk of this happening, those willing to wield weapons will be able to assert their sway. The nuclear pacifist draws the line, not at the risk of the deaths of others (in the case of a major modern war with conventional weapons, the deaths of many millions) but at the possession or use of nuclear weapons. This means that beyond a certain point those willing to wield nuclear weapons will be able to assert their sway.

Nuclear pacifism is a position favoured by a number of Christians. It is given most careful explication by the Master of Balliol College, Oxford. Anthony Kenny writes that we can avoid any nuclear attack on us 'by conceding the military or political objective of the enemy before he attacks'. Elsewhere he says that if 'there came to a point where western leaders believed that they were faced with a choice between giving in to a Soviet demand and actually using the power of nuclear devastation they had retained, they would have to choose to give in'. Again, 'there is no doubt that for a non-nuclear power blackmailed by a nuclear power the only certain way of avoiding nuclear devastation is surrender'.[9] Anthony Kenny does not underestimate the Soviet threat and he puts forward a careful programme of staged disarmament so that the threat is minimized. He is also right to suggest that there are certain circumstances when surrender, however humiliating, is the correct moral choice. But, as the quotations make clear, he is arguing for a prior and principled rejection of resistance beyond a certain point. This is not essentially different from pacifism and is open to the judgment of Ulrich Simon already quoted:

> Submission to evil powers as a policy seems to me so immoral that I had rather give up my Christian faith than subscribe to it.

Lurking behind many church statements is a crypto pacifism.[10] For this reason and despite the protests of nuclear pacifists, the whole of this chapter is relevant to the nuclear dilemma. Furthermore, whilst it is true that for deeply held moral reasons some will refuse to countenance the use of force, for no less deeply held moral reasons, as Ulrich Simon makes clear, resistance with weapons adequate to the threat is for others an overriding moral duty.[11] Nevertheless, there are other crucial considerations which have led highly respected figures in our time to become nuclear pacifists and these are discussed in Chapters Eight to Eleven.

Notes

1. John 18.23.
2. D.H. Lawrence, *The Rainbow,* Heinemann Phoenix Edition, 1957, p.282.
3. 'The bomb — a Christian enigma' in *Tracts for our Times 1833-1983* St Mary's, Bourne Street, 1983.
4. Martin Ceadel, 'Christian Pacifism in the era of the two World Wars', *The Church and War,* Ecclesiastical History Society, Blackwell, 1984.
5. John Yoder, *Nevertheless,* Herald Press, Pennsylvania, 1976.
6. T. Taylor, *Munich — The Price of Peace,* Vintage Books, NY, 1979, p.310.
7. Mark 13.32.
8. G.H.C. Macgregor, *The New Testament Basis of Pacifism,* Fellowship of Reconciliation, 1953, p.102.
9. Anthony Kenny, *The Logic of Deterrence,* Firethorn Press, 1985, pp.59, 73, 77.
10. I have analysed this in 'The Christian Churches and the pacifist temptation' in *The World Today,* Royal Institute of International Affairs, Aug.-Sept. 1984, Vol.40, Nos.8-9.
11. A more detailed examination of modern pacifism is made in my essay, 'Reinhold Niebuhr's critique of Pacifism and his pacifist critics', in *Reinhold Niebuhr and the Issues of Our Time,* ed. Richard Harries, Mowbray, 1986.

CHAPTER FIVE

Loyalty to the state and its limits

In the fourth century, under the emperor Constantine, Christianity became the official religion of the Roman empire, and there began that connection with the state which has since become so controversial. However, there is a markedly positive attitude to the state by most New Testament writers: and this is in marked contrast to the way many feel today. For in Europe since the first World War there has been in many quarters, though not in Wales, Brittany, Scotland or among the Basques, a sharp suspicion of state power and a dislike of nationalism. The reasons for this are not hard to fathom. First, one of the major factors which made the first World War possible was the unswerving loyalty to the state which was inculcated by all European governments and believed by most of their people. Children at school were taught the history of their country in glorious and patriotic terms. In Germany, as well as the explicitly militaristic Prussian culture, with its emphasis on obedience and discipline, there were the freer youth movements, the *Wandervögel* which, whilst they were set up to some extent in reaction against militarism, in fact provided opportunity for teaching about and service to the fatherland. It is impossible to understand the outbreak of World War 1 without the intense patriotism of all the major European powers.[1] The horrible, tragic carnage of the war not only called all this into question but led to a strong revulsion against it. *Dulce et decorum est pro patria mori* became 'that old lie'[2] not only for Wilfred Owen but for people right up to our own time, who have been haunted by the memory of the first World War, rather than the second. The fine literature produced by the Great War has ensured that it is the senseless futility of the trenches which has moved the imaginations of succeeding generations. The history of World War 2 reminds us of what

51

can be at stake in international politics. But often this has been overshadowed by World War 1 literature depicting the character of war.

Secondly, there has been the widespread persuasive influence of Marxist ideas. According to Lenin the state is 'an institution of violence for the suppression of some class'. Marxists reject the idea of the value-free state that liberals believe we should aim at. The state can only serve the interests of some class or other — either the bourgeoisie in capitalist societies or the proletariat in socialist societies. As far as the Churches are concerned this analysis has made them highly suspicious of government and anxious to identify with the struggling poor. In South America the traditional alliance of the Church with the rich and powerful has been broken. The church there is now, above all, concerned to identify with the poor in their struggle for liberation from social injustice.

Thirdly, there has been the assertion of liberal, humane values; an emphasis on relationship rather than big political ideas or ideologies. In a world where causes of one kind and another have led to the suffering and deaths of so many millions of uninvolved people, it has been natural for some people to eschew politics and affirm the primacy of personal values and tender human relationships. Some words which the novelist E.M. Forster wrote in 1939 become notorious because it was alleged, wrongly, that they helped to create the climate of treason in which the British spies, Burgess, Philby and Maclean could operate. Forster wrote:

> If I had to choose between betraying my country and betraying my friend, I hope I should have the guts to betray my country.[3]

Fourthly, within the limited confines of the Church of England the changing socio-economic position of the clergy has undoubtedly contributed to a different attitude to the state. For many centuries the clergy, or at least the higher clergy, of the Church of England were closely related to the ruling elite by birth and education. This is no longer the case. It means the clergy, even many higher clergy, have no natural affinity with or sympathy for, those who exercise the levers of power, especially when a Conservative government is in office. This has been one factor in the general distancing of the Church from the state.

In the face of these and other factors, such as the spread of Tolstoyan ideas, it is necessary to assert that, on a Christian view of existence, government is both natural and a necessity. As was indicated in Chapter Three, man is a social being and it is natural for him to come together with others of his fellows to organize common life for the benefit of all. Given this, it is natural, as Aquinas argued, that there should be a centre of political authority to reconcile and harmonize different interests. Government is also necessary, however, because it is only a political authority with power to coerce that can hold wayward human beings together in community. Government has to co-operate with God in ordering the unruly wills of sinful mankind. So, despite the understandable disillusionment with all forms of patriotism as a result of the first World War and the corresponding temptation to eschew the idea of government altogether, we cannot do without it. Moreover, despite the element of truth in the Marxist analysis of goverment — for it is true that government does always serve the interests of one group more than another — no government is simply the unwitting agent of a particular class. Lenin defined the state as an instiution of violence. But on a Christian view a distinction has to be made between force and violence. In common usage force may be a neutral term but technically it is the moral, legally authorized, discriminate and proportionate use of coercion. Violence is the immoral, illegal, indiscriminate or disproportionate use of coercion. Agents of the state can become violent, as when police act in an illegal way or use a disproportionate amount of coercion. Nevertheless, for the most part they exercise force, that is, coercion which is legally authorized by the state and which is a proportionate response to the threat in question. This force is not only legal but moral, because, on a Christian view, no state can exist on the basis of consent alone. The state exercises morally grounded and legitimate coercion. It is true that the state will always serve the interests of some more than others. Despite democracy, which gives some purchase to the interest of voters, there is under capitalism a bias towards the wealthy. In a communist society it is 'the new class', the members of the Communist party, the bureaucrats and their hangers on, all of whom live on the perks and privileges of those who are close to the centre of power. But both systems of government have a *prima facie* legitimacy. At the moment this is probably true even of the Soviet Union despite the essentially untruthful nature of Marxist-Leninism.

In response to the third point about the primacy of relationships over any kind of political commitment it has to be pointed out that, sadly, without a secure political order, there can be no worthwhile relationships. Where anarchy exists people are totally taken up with surviving. For these reasons, therefore, most Christians have seen the state as divinely ordered. The classical words are in Paul in his thirteenth chapter to the Romans.

> Let every person be subject to the governing authorities.
> For there is no authority except from God, and those
> that exist have been instituted by God.

Despite the suspicion which many Christians feel towards state power, and the alleged demise of nationalism, it is in fact nationalism which has proved the most powerful political idea in the twentieth century. During the first World War love of country proved a potent dissolvant of both socialist and liberal internationalism. The solidarity of the working class across national borders quickly gave way to an instinctive loyalty to the national community. Similarly, after the second World War, quarrels within the Marxist bloc have been continuously in evidence, most obviously between China and Russia, but also between the Soviet Union and the countries of eastern Europe, nearly all of whom have been anxious to affirm their independent identity. But it has been in Africa and other developing countries where the force of nationalism has been seen at its most dramatic. It has succeeded in uniting people, divided in almost every other way, into a political force capable of overthrowing the colonial regime.

There have always been some Christians suspicious of appeals of loyalty to the nation, notably Dr Johnson:

> Patriotism having become one of our topics, Johnson suddenly uttered, in a strong determined tone, an apothegm, at which many will start: 'Patriotism is the last refuge of the scoundrel.' But let it be considered, that he did not mean a real and generous love of our country, but that pretended patriotism which so many, in all ages and countries have made a cloak of self-interest.[4]

Whether Johnson really meant what Boswell thought he meant, or something more astringent, we cannot decide. Certainly, many Christians today share the scepticism of Johnson. Yet not all. In the Orthodox Church patriotism is evaluated very positively. It is true that in eastern European countries under Soviet dominance the appeal to nationalism, and the link between nationalism and the Church, serves an obvious political purpose. Central to the message of Father Jerzy Popieluszko, was the theme that God had created nations and made us part of them. The message was enough of a threat for him to be murdered. But this view is deeply embedded in Orthodox Christian thought. Solzhenitsyn has written:

> Nations are the wealth of mankind, its collective personalities; the very least of them wears its own special colours and bears within itself a special facet of divine intervention.[5]

Whilst Vadim Borisov, a Russian Orthodox historian living in the Soviet Union, quoting Dostoevsky that the nation is 'an organized being and moreover a *moral personality*', has written:

> The nation is a level in the hierarchy of the Christian cosmos, a part of God's immutable purpose. Nations are not created by a people's history. Rather, the nation's personality realizes itself through that history

or, to put it another way, the people in their history
fulfil God's design for them.[6]

This way of thinking has dangers. It can lead to an
uncritical nationalism, and can be perverted into ideas of a
master race or a nation that through its conquests is furthering
the grand design of God. Nevertheless, the fact that an idea
can be corrupted does not make it invalid, and there is an
inescapable element of truth in the viewpoint of Solzhenitsyn
and Borisov. For we find our identity, in part, through our
past, and that past includes not only the past of our own
family but the past of our race and nation. A few years ago in
the United States millions of people watched the TV series
Roots in which a black family traced its history back through
the time of slavery to its origins in West Africa. A
consciousness of where we have come from, of the community from which we have sprung, helps form our understanding of who we are. We have not been placed on the earth
devoid of all features and characteristics. We have not been
created as trans-nationals, without distinguishing features.
We have been created part of a nation, as members of a race,
and citizens of a country. To believe that creation is good, the
work of a good God who is pleased with what he has made, is
to believe also that the community into which we have been
born, by which we have been shaped and which gives us part
of our identity, has a place in the providence of God.

From the standpoint of Christian theology, therefore, it is
necessary to say: first, that membership of a political
community, and in our time this is usually a nation-state, is
not an optional extra but an inescapable precondition for
human existence; secondly, that our membership of a
particular race or nation (which will often be part of a
nation-state) will have positive as well as negative value, for it
is part of the process through which God has chosen to create
us. Nevertheless, there are limits in our allegiance to both
nation and state.

First, our loyalty to the state can never be an absolute. Only
God has our absolute allegiance. It is the constant temptation
of mankind to give our total loyalty to something finite; to
give our unqualified support, which belongs to God alone, to

something less than God. Amongst the rivals to God, in this sense, the state ranks high. But the state is, in reformation terminology, only a provisional order. It is necessary now for the conditions of life on earth, but these are passing. So there is no question of the state commanding our absolute loyalty; only God has that. Moreover, there will always be a temptation for rulers to try to obtain from their citizens an unqualified loyalty to the state; and this has to be resisted.

Secondly, there may be occasions when the state is no longer sanctioned by divine authority. The first of the conditions of the 'just war' tradition is that war can only be declared by legitimate authority, that is, the supreme governing power of the state. Yet sometimes it may become a duty not only to disobey the governing power, but also actively to resist it even to the point of armed struggle. How can this be? In particular, how can an armed struggle against one's own government fulfil the first condition of the 'just war' tradition, which says that a war must have legitimate authority behind it? The answer derives from the fact that government is based not simply on the capacity to coerce people into submission, but also on consent. This consent does not necessarily have to be expressed through democratic procedures, highly desirable though these are. A benevolent dictatorship could be a true government, that is, one to be obeyed for God's sake, if it did in fact have the unspoken and unvoted for consent, or just the aquiescence, of its people. But sometimes it may become clear that a particular non-democratic system does not have the support of the majority of the people. The classic example of this in recent times was the rule of the Shah of Iran. He had all the panoply of government, a vast army and police force. He appeared securely in control. Yet one exiled voice, that of the Ayatollah Khomeini, was able to appeal to the people and overthrow the Shah in a comparatively bloodless revolution. This was only possible because, despite all the trapping of state power, the people had in fact withdrawn their consent. The Shah's government no longer had legitimate authority, which had passed to others. An equally dramatic recent example was the overthrow of President Marcos in the Philippines by Mrs Aquino and the unarmed populace. Clearly this raises questions. What signs are there that this authority no longer resides with those who claim to be the government? Is it not a highly dangerous idea, for any small group can resist any government on this basis? Yet, despite the lack of objective criteria for when a government has in fact ceased to be the morally authorized government, and despite the dangers, the Iranian and Philippine examples make it clear that such a situation has happened and can in principle happen again.

The approach just outlined makes use of an assumption of political philosophy that true government is rooted in the consent of the people. There is also another, more biblical, approach which leads to the same conclusion. It is one developed by the German Lutheran Theologian, Helmut Thielicke, in the aftermath of the Nazi experience. It has often been said that the rise to unbridled power of the Nazis in Germany was in part made possible by the tradition of unquestioning obedience to the state; and this in turn was nourished by the heavy emphasis in Lutheran theology on Paul's statement in Romans 13 that the state is authorized by God. Thielicke has argued that Romans 13 is not the only text in the New Testament that bears on the problem of obedience. There is also Revelation 13. Revelation 13 is about the great beast, and the great beast is a state which has become demonic. A state becomes demonic when it arrogates to itself the functions of God by seeking to control all aspects of human life. When a state begins to act like this, seeking control over all areas of life, it ceases to be the state of Romans 13, which we are enjoined to obey, and it becomes the great beast described in Revelation 13, which we are duty bound to resist. It ceases to be the divinely ordained state of Romans 13 and ceases to have authority over us. It has usurped the place of God and must be resisted.

There is, then, no question of any state having absolute authority over us, and circumstances may come about, however difficult to define in advance, in which a particular government loses its claim to divine legitimacy. Nevertheless, there is within the Christian tradition a great caution about pursuing this line of thought too far. For if human beings are sinful, then nothing could be worse than a state of total anarchy with human beings devouring their neighbours like wild beasts. There is in Christian tradition, a constant worry about 'the mischief of setting things afloat'; constant warnings that the medicine might prove worse than the disease and new forms of tyranny arise more oppresive than the overthrown regime. An extreme but not uncharacteristic statement of this fear was expressed by William Tyndale, who argued that a ruler, 'though he is the greatest tyrant in the world, yet is he unto thee a great benefit. It is better to have something than to be strip out altogether.' Indeed a tyrant is better than a weak king, for 'it is better to suffer one tyrant than many, and to suffer wrong of one than of every man'.

Strictly speaking, these considerations come under the criteria known as the principle of proportion, which is considered in later chapters. They appear here to indicate the extent of the caution felt by most Christian writers about calling the authority of the state into question. Nor was their caution unjustified.

There are strict limits to the authority of the state. It may become demonic, as it did in Nazi Germany. It may not rest on the consent of the people, as in South Africa today where the black majority do not play any part in the political process. So a Christian might be led to refuse to serve in the South African armed forces or even to join into the armed struggle against the regime. It may be that one particular aspect of Government policy is judged immoral, as some judge the possession of nuclear weapons to be. This leads them to refuse to pay a percentage of their tax or to acts of deliberate civil disobedience. Nevertheless, despite the limits on state authority, it has a *prima facie* authority which all citizens are bound to respect. This authority of the state can lead to the tragic situation where people of good will, believing in the same God, can find themselves on opposite sides in a war. What appalled the liberal Christian conscience as much as anything about World War 1, and led to a revulsion against all forms of patriotism, was the sight of so many young men on both sides, believing in God, thinking their country was right, going to their own death and taking others with them. We feel the same today about a war that is in some respects similar, that between Iran and Iraq, where thousands of young men and children, inspired by their faith or their patriotism and manipulated by their rulers, are going to their deaths on both sides.

The 'just war' tradition has been aware of this dilemma ever since it admitted that people could be subjectively innocent even though fighting in an unjust cause. At its origins the 'just war' tradition tended to think of war exclusively in terms of the punishment of the wicked by the just. As it was also asserted that soldiers and citizens have a duty to obey their governments, then clearly that position becomes untenable. But here we come face to face with one of the tragic dimensions of life, that people doing what they ought to do, obeying their government, find themselves caught up, killing and being killed, for an unjust cause. Here we go beyond ethics into theology.

First, though we rightly admire the courageous individual who stands out against the state and opposes it, even at the cost of his own life, there is also another course of action, no less admirable; the way of identification, of solidarity. No one was more aware of the futility of the first World War than Wilfred Owen, yet when he was in England recovering from wounds, he felt he had to go back to the trenches. Although he had an intuition that he would be killed, he felt something calling him to go back and be with his men. If he was to speak for them he had to be with them:

> I heard the sighs of men, that have no skill
> To speak of their distress, no, nor the will!
> A voice I know. And this time I must go.[7]

Bonhoeffer put the point even more eloquently and clearly. He could have stayed out of Germany. Instead, as he wrote to Reinhold Niebuhr:

> I shall have no right to participate in the reconstruction of Christian life in Germany after the war if I do not share the trials of this time with my people . . . Christians in Germany will face the terrible alternative of either willing the defeat of their nation in order that Christian civilization may survive, or willing the

victory of their nation and thereby destroying our civilization. I know which of these alternatives I must choose; but I cannot make this choice in security.[8]

This sense by Owen and Bonhoeffer, that they wished to be with their people and share their predicament and confusion, is rooted in the profound principle of incarnation. God became incarnate, sharing our life to the full. The redemption he wrought was not from on high but from within the process. A similar instinct may lead a person to stay with his country, even though he has severe doubts about the rightness of his country's cause.

There is an inescapably tragic dimension to life and the Christian faith offers resources to cope with life because that tragic dimension is included in the faith itself, in the cross, in the killing of the Son of God by the sons of God. It offers hope, even in the midst of tragedy, that the tragic is not the last word. It can therefore cope with a situation in which, as has often happened in the past, people who believe in the same God, in the one Lord Jesus Christ, have been caught up on opposite sides of a war.

There are courageous Christians who believe with a deep sense of conviction that any and every way is totally contrary to the will of God, who for this reason oppose the state and are willing if necessary to suffer the consequences of their stand. There are others who believe that a particular state has become demonic, or that it has become involved in an unjust war, and for such reasons they also defy the state and are willing to suffer for it. But there have been many other Christians, the majority, who for a mixture of reasons have fought for their country and died for it, in a war which in retrospect may seem to be wrong or futile. The Christian faith has a word of hope to say to them too. This is not to sidestep ethical judgements about particular wars in the past, or wars that might have to be fought in the future. It is to suggest that ethics has its proper place within the wider perspective of theology. That perspective will include a proper loyalty to one's community, a sense of the tragic and a conviction that, despite the tragic dimension, the purpose of God for us will ultimately prevail. These theological considerations are taken up again in the last chapter. The point, for the present stage of the argument, is that the state has a *prima facie* claim on our loyalty, even when it summons us to military service.[9] It is sad that so few in the past have refused to serve in unjust wars. It is deeply disappointing that only a handful in South Africa today refuse military service for a manifestly unjust regime fighting an illegal and unjust war in Namibia. Yet, in principle, the state has a claim upon us.

Notes

1. James Joll, *The Origins of the First World War,* Longmans, 1984, Chapter 8.
2. 'Dulce et Decorum est' in *Wilfred Owen, War Poems and Others,* ed. Dominic Hibberd, Chatto and Windus, 1975, p.79.
3. E.M. Forster, 'What I believe' in *Two Cheers for Democracy,* Edward Arnold, 1951, p.78.
4. Boswell's *Life of Dr Johnson,* 7 April 1775.
5. L. Labedz, *Solzhenitsyn: A Documentary Record,* 1974, p.314.
6. V. Borisov, 'Personality and National awareness', in A. Solzhenitsyn (ed) *From Under the Rubble,* 1975, p.209.
7. 'The Calls', Wilfred Owen, *War Poems and Others,* p.100.
8. Letter to Reinhold Niebuhr, quoted in article by Niebuhr in *Union Seminary Quarterly Review,* Vol.1, no.3, March 1946, p.3.
9. I have written more fully about the state and just revolution in *Should a Christian support Guerrillas?,* Lutterworth, 1982.

CHAPTER SIX

Christian Obedience and the Just War Tradition

During the first two centuries of the Church's existence most Christians were reluctant, for a variety of reasons, to join the Roman army. When Constantine became Emperor, much changed, and by the year 410 the army had become a closed shop for Christians. The Church blessed God for the *Pax Romana* and saw in it the fulfilment of the prophecies of peace contained in the Old Testament. It is true that some Christians on the edge of the empire did not see it in these terms, notably the Donatists in North Africa. But the vast majority saw the empire as providential and had no difficulty supporting it by prayer and the sword. Some Christians now regard what happened under Constantine as the great betrayal, the time when the Church sold its soul and, in return for its position of privilege, gave state power a religious sanction.

The matter can, however, be looked at very differently, as a time when the Church grew up and assumed its fair share of responsibility for the ordering of the common life we all share. No doubt this was not possible when the Church was a small, persecuted and heavenward looking sect. But, when under Constantine it had the opportunity, which it took, of sharing in the exercise of coercive power and being tainted with the associated guilt, it showed a proper maturity. For we live in society, and society needs political control. It is not for the Church which cares for the conditions under which men live and which serves a master who did not scruple to mix with both soldiers and collaborators, to disassociate itself from those who exercise power. The Church is indeed concerned with the city of God. But on this earth it shares with all men the conditions of life without which there can be no earthly pilgrimage. As St Augustine put it:

> Thus, the heavenly City, so long as it is wayfaring on earth, not only makes use of earthly peace but fosters and actively pursues along with other human beings a common platform in regard to all that concerns our purely human life . . .[1]

It was during the fourth and fifth centuries, particularly under the influence of Augustine, but also Ambrose who baptized him, that the Church began to consider more carefully the conditions under which it might be morally right to go to war. This has now come to be called the 'just war' tradition. It is not a static body of thought but has been subject to continuous modification and development over the centuries in response to different historical circumstances. Nevertheless, there is a remarkable degree of continuity in the principles that have been taught. As now received by us, the tradition may be divided into two main parts. First, the moral considerations that arise when deciding whether or not to go to war *(ius ad bellum)*. Secondly, the morality of the conduct of the war *(ius in bello)*.

The main conditions that must be fulfilled for a war to be called just are as follows.

1. It must be declared by supreme authority. When two citizens have a dispute they can go to a court that will arbitrate between them. If one of them is dissatisfied by the judgment he can appeal against it right up to the highest court in the land, which will then make a final decision. But there is no supreme international authority able both to make and to enforce a decision. Although all countries pay lip service to the United Nations, if a matter of vital national interest is in dispute and the UN is failing to resolve the matter in a way that is satisfactory, the government of a country that feels aggrieved may well feel, on moral grounds, that force has to be used, even though in so doing it violates the charter. Below the level of government, disputes can be resolved; in the end, by government itself. Between governments there is not, at the moment, any effective arbitration. So govern-

ments retain the right to defend themselves; which is usually stretched in practice to the right to defend their vital interests and those of their allies.

2. The cause must be just. According to the UN charter, there is now only one just cause, and that is the right to defend oneself if attacked. The 'just war' tradition, however, never limited just cause to wars of defence only. There could be a just war of offence to recover territory that had been lost, or more generally to right a grievous wrong. The British war to recover the Falklands, for example: is it to be seen as a war of defence, or as a war to recover territory that had been lost? More controversially, the United States invasion of Grenada could not be ruled out *per se* by the Just War tradition.

3. War must be a last resort. Every effort must have been made to resolve the crisis by peaceful means.

4. The expected war must not inflict more harm than would otherwise be suffered. (The principle of proportion.)

5. There must be a reasonable chance of success. This is, in fact, an extension of the previous condition. Luther, for example, said that it was absurd and immoral to go to war against the Turk, with a much smaller, ill-equipped army, in which defeat would be likely; for this would simply bring about even greater suffering.

6. The war must be fought with the right intention. It must be waged with a view to establishing a just peace.

The two main moral conditions that must be observed in the conduct of the war *(ius in bello)* are as follows.

1. Non-combatants must not be the direct and intentional object of attack.

2. An attack on a particular target must be proportionate: i.e. if Britain had used nuclear weapons against the Argentinian mainland in order to recapture the Falklands, most people would have judged this disproportionate.

It is obvious that every one of these conditions raises many questions and there has been much debate over the centuries as to what exactly each of them means. For example, there have been disputes as to how likely success has to appear before a war can be held to be just. Does it have to appear near certain? Or just probable? Or will an even chance of victory be enough? Furthermore, what counts as success? Revolutionary wars, for example, do not count on big military victories. Revolutionary war is primarily a political struggle, and what counts as success is staying in the field, being enough of a nuisance, until the political victory has been won. Again, it has been doubted whether these conditions apply in a war of defence. If it is a life or death struggle even to survive, in the face of a direct attack, some hold that it is the moral thing to do to fight even if the odds against the victory are overwhelming.

Two of the principles, which are crucial in a nuclear age, the principle of proportion (which appears under both *ius in bello* and *ius ad bellum)* and the principle of discrimination, which says that non-combatants must not be the object of direct attack, are the subject of extended discussion in later chapters. First, however, some more general points about the 'just war' tradition, in view of the still widespread misunderstandings about it that abound.

First, it is not primarily a way of justifying war. No doubt that is the use to which it has most often been put. But it is no less meant to be a check on going to war. Its basic assumption is that war is a very terrible thing and can only be justified for the most serious reasons. It asks whether the reason is really serious enough. It assumes that there is a *prima facie* case against going to war, and puts the burden of proof on those who claim that in this particular instance it can be justified.

Secondly, it is sometimes said today that the 'just war' tradition has been rendered obsolete by the advent of nuclear weapons. It no longer applies. Nothing could be further from the truth. For the very judgement that some might make, for example that any use of nuclear weapons would be disproportionate and could not be justified by any conceivable good, is a judgement using one of the canons of the 'just war' tradition. There are two ways in which a person can make a judgement that a particular war is immoral. He can do so on pacifist grounds; for the reason that all war is immoral. Or he can give reasons why this particular war, or kind of warfare, is immoral. Those reasons will be drawn from the long tradition of thought on this subject that goes under the name of the 'just war' tradition.

Thirdly, although the 'just war' tradition has in the main

been developed by Christian theologians, there is nothing distinctively Christian about it. The origin of the tradition lies with the Greeks, many years before Christ. From the time of Grotius in the sixteenth century, the tradition became just as much part of international law as it was of moral theology. In its early stages, *ius in bello* owed much to the professional ethic of the knightly class and, in its later stages, it became enshrined not only in international law but in the military manuals of most countries in the world. So, although the tradition of moral thinking by theologians is clearly discernable, it built upon, responded to, and fed into, the work of people whose prime interest was in law or the practical business of fighting. For some, the fact that there is nothing distinctively Christian about the 'just war' tradition rules it out from the start. And some of the grave suspicion that it arouses today amongst Christians is because they hanker after a distinctively Christian stance, a clear Christian contribution to this subject which is radically different from secular morality. Hence, people are attracted, rightly, to the person of Jesus and the possibility of a stance on war that is radically different, so it is held, from the tired, compromised thinking of men of affairs.

It has to be admitted that at this point fundamental disagreements about the foundation and nature of Christian ethics are bound to arise. The position taken here is that all people, whatever their religious beliefs or lack of them, have a sense of right and wrong; that there is a morality common to humanity as such. And that, whatever the effects of 'the fall', it is still possible for human beings to discern that some things are right and others wrong. This approach can be subsumed under the general heading of 'natural law' thinking, an approach which was out of favour for many years but which has shown some signs of being rehabilitated in a modified form. The 'just war' tradition belongs within the overall sphere of natural law thinking. In other words, anyone concerned to think seriously about the morality of warfare would, whatever their religious presuppositions, see that these conditions apply. You do not have to be a Christian to see that not anyone should be allowed to wage war, but only those to whom has been committed authority to defend their country. You do not have to be a Christian to see that war should be waged not for any cause but only one that is just; that war should be waged only as a very last resort and not for any pretext. The fact that these conditions can be seen to apply by anyone of good will is not detrimental to the Christian faith. First, for the most part, it has been Christian theologians who have developed them. Secondly, the whole thrust of the 'just war' tradition is to bring the sphere of war into the sphere of morality and to curtail the occasions on which war can be waged and to limit the damage which it inflicts. This is not distinctively Christian but it is certainly a concern that Christians, along with others, should be engaged in. Thirdly, there is an emphasis not only on public morality but on the morality of the individual and his or her motivation. War is to be waged with the right intention, not for aggrandizement or even honour but for a just peace. The whole thrust and spirit of the 'just war' tradition, whilst not exclusively Christian, is properly Christian.

The 'just war' tradition, although developed by Christians, can appeal to the common conscience of mankind and as such belongs within the sphere of natural law thinking. In particular it concerns the conditions of life which all people share, Christians included. Christians share with others the need for human community and a political authority to hold that community together. As St Augustine put it, Christians pursue 'along with other human beings, a common platform in regard to all that concerns our purely human life'. Christians set this common platform within the wider context of the goal of heavenly peace within the City of God and they set it under the ultimate judgement of the standard of that city, revealed in Christ. But for life in this world there is often a common platform and the 'just war' tradition is part of this.

Fourthly, the 'just war' tradition exists to insist that morality is applicable to war, as to everything else in human life. For, if the criticism from some quarters is that there is nothing distinctively Christian about the 'just war' tradition, the assertion from elsewhere is that morality has no place in war. This assertion takes two forms. One, less fashionable now, is that states should be governed only by *realpolitik,* by what is in their own interests, and that moral considerations have no part to play. If it is in the interest of a state to go to war, it should do so. This, of course, the 'just war' tradition totally rejects. It asserts that a state can only go to war for the very gravest moral reasons when there is absolutely no other alternative. Secondly, there is the view, more frequently expressed, that once war is declared, 'anything goes'. People who take this view are often highly concerned that war should not break out but they believe that if it does, moral considerations simply cease to apply. War, they declare, is an appalling, brutal business and it must be won and brought to an end as quickly as possible by any means possible. It was a view sometimes expressed during the second World War and also during the war in Vietnam. It is a view directed against the whole *ius in bello* part of the Christian 'just war' tradition. Against such a view the *ius in bello* tradition, together with a great deal of international and military law, asserts that even in the midst of war man remains a moral being and that only what is strictly necessary to the achievement of legitimate goals may be done.

Fifthly, the 'just war' tradition assumes a particular view of life. This view was outlined in Chapter Three. It assumes that the world is now and always will be a place of conflict; conflict which will always be at risk of erupting into actual war. It assumes that there might be occasions when states are tempted to fight wars for trivial or immoral reasons, and therefore they have to be warned on moral grounds against this. It also assumes, however, that there might be occasions when a state has to fight a war, for the best moral reasons, because of some unjust aggression by others. The 'just war' tradition exists, and must continue to exist, because rulers will always be tempted to fight unjust wars. And, because sometimes they yield to this temptation, men must fight just wars against them.

No less than this, however, the 'just war' tradition assumes that life will go on after the war is over; that life can and must return to a state in which, although there will be continuing conflict, this conflict will be expressed in ways other than war. The two most significant symbols of this are the custom of diplomatic immunity and the ancient taboo against the poisoning of wells. The existence of diplomatic immunity, however often it may be abused, is a symbol that states wish to relate to one another even during a period of conflict. If war actually breaks out diplomats leave enemy territory. But before that point they are a sign that states have to relate to one another despite conflicts of interest. The ancient taboo against the poisoning of wells was a dramatic warning that the conditions which make life possible must not be destroyed. War took place, it was felt, in order that life might exist on a more satisfactory basis; it must not result in the destruction of life altogether.

The 'just war' tradition assumes a view of existence which is strongly anti-utopian, and it regards all forms of utopianism as a dangerous illusion. Instead of thinking of human beings as basically peace-loving and of life as a peaceful state which has gone temporarily wrong, it suggests something more shocking and sombre. It assumes that life is struggle and conflict and that this conflict is always on the edge of breaking out into war. Instead of dreaming dreams of a world once and for all free of the plague of war, it acknowledges that war is always a possibility and seeks to limit the number of occasions in which a war may be fought. Furthermore, working on the assumption that a war is always likely to take place, it is concerned to keep any ensuing destruction to a minimum. Human beings are always prone to utopian dreams, and indeed these have an important place; but when they are treated as realizable schemes the result is dangerous. Utopianism is not confined to some pacifists. President Reagan's Strategic Defence Initiative, which holds out the hope of totally abolishing the threat of nuclear weapons, is as utopian as the dream of general and complete disarmament. Both distract from the real issue which is: 'How, in a world of perpetual conflict and of radically opposed ideologies, armed to the teeth, do we stop war actually breaking out? Within the overall context of a balance of power which ensures that the cost of war to any potential aggressor would be too high, the obvious answer is, by a great deal more attention to crisis management and confidence building measures; and by such things as ensuring that the hot line is working, that there are procedures to stop misunderstandings and miscalculations over incidents that are bound to occur from time to time, as when a missile being used in exercises goes off course and flies over the boundaries of neighbouring countries. These are practical, rather than moral considerations. The point is, however, that the frame of mind, the mentality, which is expressed in the 'just war' tradition, is the kind of mentality that is concerned with such nuts and bolts. Its concern is not to eliminate all possibility of war, which it regards as an unattainable goal under the conditions of human existence, but to stop particular wars, which are liable to break out, from actually breaking out.

For this reason those who stand in the 'just war' tradition will regard themselves as neither doves nor hawks but owls. Owls are concerned with the irrational factors that bring wars about; the accidents, the misreading of situations, the political miscalculations.

Sixthly, it might be argued that 'just war' thinking, however sound in theory, is of no practical use. Those who have wanted to wage war in the past have either ignored the guidelines altogether or stretched them to accommodate what they intended to do anyway. Similarly, a point particularly relevant to the discussion in subsequent chapters, once a war has broken out all restraints are brushed aside either deliberately or in the heat of battle. It is beyond the scope of this study to examine the effect of 'just war' principles on past conduct but two general points can be made. First, 'just war' principles have often come to be expressed in international conventions and military codes. Though sometimes ignored, these have, more often than not, been enforced and are in principle enforceable. Secondly, even if it could be shown that 'just war' criteria had in practice been almost totally ignored it would still be important both to reflect on the morality of force and to try to draw up guidelines. For the alternative would be that the deployment of force belonged to a totally amoral realm outside the rest of human activity. That alternative is quite unacceptable. Therefore we need to continue thinking about both *ius ad bellum* and *ius in bello*. This is all part of the process of creating a moral consensus among mankind on this most crucial of issues; and even if ignored a million times it would still be important to go on working at it. In fact, in the modern era, there is perhaps a greater chance than in the past of enforcing at least some of the moral restraints. For there is a more developed system of international law and international machinery for enforcing it than ever before. 'Just war' thinking seeks to contribute to the moral consensus out of which international conventions come and as a result of which they are observed.

Finally, there is another misconception about the 'just war' tradition that must be corrected. This is partly semantic. The word 'just' carried overtones of confidence: in this context, of moral confidence, perhaps even self-righteousness and a refusal to question one's own moral position. The word 'just' is also related to 'justify', so that it might be thought that in fighting a just war one was thereby justified. These are semantic confusions but the issue goes deeper than this. Some Christians who stress the fact that we are justified by faith and not by works are not only suspicious of 'works of righteousness' but also of any attempt to give Christian guidance as to what might be the right or just course of action in any set of circumstances. But the two questions, 'How do we find acceptance with God?' and 'How do we discover what we ought to do?' are quite separate. The kind of guidance that the 'just war' tradition offers is in no way intended as a route to heaven. We are, to use the language of Luther and Paul, justified only by God's grace and our acceptance of this grace in faith. We are accepted in Christ, in the beloved. We do not strive to make ourselves acceptable to God, for he takes us, in Christ, as we are. Nevertheless, this said, there is still an urgent need for Christian guidance on a whole range of issues. This, on one issue, the 'just war' tradition seeks to give.

The Christian ethic is a theological ethic, that is, it is grounded in the being and will of God. The Christian seeks to do the will of God. 'Thy will be done on earth as it is in heaven'. More than that, the being and will of God have been revealed in Christ. So that, when Paul wants to inculcate humility, he points his readers to the humility of God in the incarnation. When he wants to urge generosity, he points to the fact that Christ, for our sake, became poor. For the Christian it is not only a duty to do the will of God, it has become his delight: for this will has been shown in all its beauty as good will towards us, and we have been won over to it. It is our duty and our joy to respond to God as he has revealed himself in Christ, and to seek his will. The question arises, however, as to how we discover his will; not so that in the doing of it we may find acceptance with God, for that we already have, but that we may, for the love of him, find it and do it. The question of how we discover the will of God again raises the fundamental questions of moral philosophy and theology, and takes us beyond the scope of this book. But, on this issue, pacifists tend to focus on the New Testament, in particular on the sermon on the mount, whilst the 'just war' tradition looks also to the reasoning of the human mind and the common conscience of mankind. Whilst this diversity cannot be disregarded, reflecting as it does different under-standings of the nature of revelation and authority, one fundamental factor, at the heart of the whole enterprise, should not be overlooked. Christians of all persuasions are trying to exercise a loving obedience to the will of God in Christ. There may be much dispute as to the form this obedience should take. What should not be in dispute is that we are trying to discover what obedience to Christ means in this very difficult area of war and peace.

For reasons indicated in earlier chapters, the will of God for us cannot simply be read off from the sermon on the mount, or even the Gospels. The whole New Testament, with its reflection of the tension between Christ's rising and his coming again, has to be taken into account. Furthermore, we cannot separate the New Testament from the Old. Christ assumed the Old Testament, and Paul taught that Christ himself was mystically present in the experience of the people of the Old Covenant. 'For they drank from the supernatural rock which followed them, and the rock was Christ.'[2] Nor can Christ's mystical, anonymous presence be limited to the people of the Old Testament. When John in the prologue to his Gospel speaks of the word becoming flesh, the word of which he speaks is 'The true light that enlightens every man'. Despite the darkness of our corrupt wills and beclouded minds, 'the light shines in the darkness'. This light is the logos or word that is present in both the moral imperative that confronted the prophets of the Old Testament, and also in the word of rational integrity in the light of which the Greeks tried to think. Finally, there is also the light of the Holy Spirit, guiding the Church into all truth. Whilst the 'just war' tradition has certainly not been kept from error, its cumulative wisdom over nearly two thousand years must in some sense have been under the guidance of the Holy Spirit, if we believe in the Holy Spirit at all.

It would be easy if the Christian, seeking obedience to the mind of Christ, could simply call up a slogan. But this would limit Christ. His mind comes to us not just through one part of the Bible but through the Bible as a whole; and not only through the Bible but from his Holy Spirit as we try to think about those matters ourselves; and through the wisdom of others who have thought about them, both in the past and today.

The 'just war' tradition offers guidance, not justification. Those who believe they are fighting a just war are still frail, fallible, sinful human beings. Reinhold Niebuhr once remarked ironically how lucky he was to find himself fighting two just wars in his lifetime. By this he meant to bring out the element of unjustness, of unrighteousness, in even the most just cause. No war is the war of the unsullied just against the unjust. All wars are between two sets of sinful human beings; but for one side it may be a duty to fight. Yet, even for the side that seems clearly in the right, not all right is on their side. Reinhold Niebuhr himself brought this out very well, not only in his writings but in the prayers he used during the second World War. Part of one prayer reads:

> We pray for the victims of tyranny, that they may resist oppression with courage. We pray for wicked and cruel men, whose arrogance reveals to us what the sin of our own hearts is like when it has conceived and brought forth its final fruit.
>
> We pray for ourselves who live in peace and quietness, that we may not regard our good fortune as proof of our virtue, or rest content to have our ease at the price of other men's sorrow and tribulation.[3]

No one has been fiercer that Reinhold Niebuhr in rejecting moral relativism and in urging that, despite the fact that everything appears grey, we still have to choose. Yet, as these prayers clearly convey, in no way does this necessarily lead to a sense of self-righteousness or to a consciousness of a war of the just against the unjust. There is a tragic element in human life and all is flawed. We have to choose, however difficult it is to distinguish between two evils, and the 'just war' tradition offers us some guidance on how to make the choice; but this is guidance not justification. Sometimes the criteria of the 'just war' tradition have seemed too neat and pat. They could suggest that God's will can be easily discovered by following these rules. No doubt this is part of the reason why people like Niebuhr and Luther have not been sympathetic towards it. They have had a strong sense of the tragic in life. Nevertheless, even if the formal conditions of the 'just war' tradition are eschewed, as with Luther, the kind of criteria that will in fact be used to think about the morality of war will inevitably be those related to the rejected tradition. This was certainly so of both Niebuhr and Luther.

All Christians seek obedience to the mind of Christ. This obedience is to be worked out in a world of conflict, a world that is always liable to slide over the edge into war. It is a tragic world, a world in which justice is never wholly on one side; but it is nevertheless a world in which choices have to be made. The 'just war' tradition offers some guidance on those choices, not as a way of being just, but as a way of trying to enter into the mind of God in Christ.

Notes

1. Augustine, *The City of God,* Book XIX, Chapter 17.
2. 1 Corinthians 10.4.
3. *Reinhold Niebuhr, Justice and Mercy,* ed. Ursula Niebuhr, Harper, 1964, p.99.

CHAPTER SEVEN

Non-combatant immunity: its origins and status

In recent decades it has been generally accepted that the principle of non-combatant immunity, or the principle of discrimination as it is sometimes called, is a cardinal principle of the 'just war' tradition. This rule states that those not directly engaged in the fighting, or not contributing to the *military* aspect of the war effort, must not be the object of *direct* attack. In other words, according to this definition munition workers could be directly attacked, but tailors and bakers could not.

The principle emerged, as a formal ethical rule, rather late in the tradition. It was only with the Spanish Dominican, Francisco de Vitoria (1480-1546) who was appalled by the suffering of the Indians in South America at the hands of the Spanish, that it was put forward with authority and clarity. Vitoria's position may be stated thus.

1. A state may take all necessary steps to defend itself. 'In war everything is lawful which the defence of the common weal requires.'[1]

2. This includes killing the fleeing enemy, punishing the inhabitants of a captured city and bombarding a fortified town, even though these actions might result in loss of life amongst women and children. Even though it is known that innocent people are likely to be killed by 'cannon and other engines of war' when a city is stormed, such action may be legitimate. 'The proof is that war could not otherwise be waged against even the guilty and the justice of the belligerents would be balked.'[2] Nevertheless, this said, there are some vital qualifications.

3. The innocent are not to be the prime object of the attack. Vitoria's contribution was to spell out clearly, for the first

time, the objective criteria for distinguishing these innocent. The crucial question is whether the person is an actual, present threat. 'All persons who are able to bear arms should be considered as injurious, since it is presumed that they are defending the king who is our enemy. It is permissible to slay them, unless . . . it is manifest that they are not injurious.'[3]

Those who are not injurious include:

(a) children,

(b) women, including the women of unbelievers,

(c) 'harmless agricultural folk' in Christian lands,

(d) the peaceable civilian population in Christian lands,

(e) foreigners and guests sojourning amongst the enemy,

(f) clerics and members of religious orders.

All these are to be presumed innocent, unless the contrary can be shown 'as when they engage in actual fighting'. It is not lawful to kill anyone on the grounds that they might constitute a threat in the future.[4]

(g) Soldiers, after victory has been won. Vitoria holds that, although a war can be just on one side only, the soldiers fighting an unjust cause might be subjectively innocent because they have a duty to obey their ruler. 'The fault of a war is usually to be laid at the door of princes — subjects fight in good faith and it is unjust they should suffer for the folly of their rulers.'[5] Hence, once freedom from the enemy is assured and those who are clearly guilty have been punished, other soldiers can be freed. 'If the innocence of any soldier is evident and the soldiers can let him go free, they are bound to do so.'[6]

Whatever the tensions set up by Vitoria's twin emphases and the difficulty of relating them to one another in practice, the principles themselves are clear enough. (1) A state may take all steps necessary to defend itself and punish the guilty, even though this may lead to the loss of innocent life. (2) Only what is strictly necessary to this aim may be done. Those who are no threat, i.e. the unarmed, must not be the object of attack. War must not be waged to the ruin of the enemy, and when victory has been won it must be utilised with moderation and to the least degree of calamity for the offending state, bearing in mind that the fault is likely to be that of the rulers, not the people.

Vitoria's teaching on non-combatant immunity is made up

of two strands. First, there is the moral principle, stated by Aquinas, that the innocent should not be deliberately killed. Secondly, there are the customary restraints on war, the lists of people who should be protected, which was part of the European culture that Vitoria inherited. Vitoria's contribution was to bring these two strands together, to define the innocent in terms of those not presenting a warlike threat, such as women and children. Vitoria's achievement was a major one. He defines clearly for the first time, the principles upon which immunity is based; but, nevertheless, there were important customary restraints before his time.

The most determined attempt in Europe to protect certain classes of people from the ravages of war came from movements in France in the tenth and eleventh centuries, known as the peace of God and the truce of God.[7] In the tenth century the Carolingian monarchy had declined, and local strong men began to assert themselves. The authority they held from the king they exercised for their own benefit. In particular, they became a threat to the Church, coveting its lands and its high offices for their placement. In response, the Church itself began to assume the responsibility which previously had belonged to the king, namely the protection of church property and personnel and the protection of the poor. At the same time, there was a sense of general expectation that the end of the world might come with the millennium of Christ's passion. The Church called on people to repent and purify themselves and to help prepare for the kingdom. Vast assemblies were held, which began in Aquitaine, and by 1033 had reached the northern frontiers of France, 'for the purpose of reforming the peace and the institution of the holy faith'. Councils were held, such as the one at Charroux in 989, where three types of violence were curbed and the perpetrators punished with anathema, those who violated the Church, those who struck an unarmed member of the clergy and those who despoiled 'a peasant or other poor man'. This protective function, previously exercised by the king was now, with a weak monarchy and rising brutal lay power, taken on by the Church.

The exercise of this function coincided with a wide desire for reformation and renewal, including the renewal of the clergy. Previously, whereas those entering monasteries had laid aside their arms, there had been no shortage of helmeted prelates and canons. Now the clergy as a class were called on to give up their arms. At the same time the *milites,* those citizens who were allowed to fight, became a more distinctive class. They were only allowed, however, to fight members of their own class. The *agricultores* and the *villani* were not to be attacked, and to these people were added, by the vows of peace in 1023–25, merchants, pilgrims and noblewomen. What these groups had in common was that they were unarmed, *'multitudo inermis vulgi'.* And the clergy were called on to be like the poor, namely unarmed. As such they were exempt from direct attack. If, however, they were armed, they became legitimate objects of attack for the *milites.*

The peace of God merged with the truce of God. Not only was there to be a social pact to limit violence, but also there was to be a pact with God to purify and prepare for the kingdom. The *milites* were called on to play their part in this truce, by refraining from fighting in Lent and on holy days and to consecrate their weapons to the service of God. (When a knight had given up his arms for Lent he too was protected.) The truce of God had a double effect. It limited violence in Europe and it directed the energies of the military class towards the infidel. The knightly class were called on both to protect the poor and fight for the faith. Pope Urban, at the Council of Clermont in 1095, exhorted them to desist from wicked combats against fellow Christians and to fight a righteous war against the enemies of the faith.

The lists of those to be protected from war found their way into the massive compilation of canon law drawn up about 1140 by Gratian, known as the *Decretum*[8]. The same groups were mentioned in Canon 22 of the third Lateran Council in 1179, which was included in the decretals, or papal decrees of Pope Gregory in the thirteenth century. Those people known as the Decretalists, canonists who commented on papal teaching in the thirteenth century, do not add much, but their repeated condemnation of the marauding gangs of mercenaries who roamed Europe and their indiscriminate violence, takes for granted the immunity of the categories mentioned in Gratian's *Decretum* and the compilations of canon law. In *De*

Treuga et pace (Of truces and peace), one of the works which added to the growing body of canon law under Pope Gregory IX in the thirteenth century, eight classes of person are listed as having full security against the ravages of war. This list includes those whose vocation forbade them from taking part in war and therefore gave them a corresponding immunity from it, such as religious and clerics, as well as pilgrims, travellers, merchants and peasants cultivating their soil (their land was also protected).

The pronouncements of the synods in the period of the peace of God and truce of God found their way not only into the canon law of the Church but into the chivalric code of the military profession. The professional ethic of the military class drew on a number of sources, but one important one was this church teaching. One of the most widely read and influential chivalric treatises during the hundred years was by a member of the Benedictine order, Honoré Bonet, who was knowledgeable in canon and civil law.[9] His book was taken by soldiers as a work on chivalry. Bonet argued for the protection not only of clerics and pilgrims but those who are too powerless to take arms, such as the widow, the orphan and poor. He appealed to kings to enforce the immunity of such people from the ravages of war on the grounds of 'worthy chivalry' and 'the ancient customs of noble warriors'. He also offered reasons for extending the list; e.g. if a poor man had only an ass to plough his land, then the ass was protected by the immunity traditionally given to the ox. Another writer in this tradition was Christine de Pisan (1361–1431). In her popular and influential work, which was read into the early sixteenth century, she argues that the poor, no more than clerics, meddle in war, and so they too ought to be left alone. With her, 'just war' teaching about the immunity of particular classes because of their vocation, e.g. clerics, converges with the chivalric ideal of protection for the poor.

The law of arms was a wonderful ideal — one ethical code transcending nationality, so that a soldier might appeal, with some hope, to an enemy commander for a rule to be observed. Yet, in reality, it may have protected only the military classes and those who could pay substantial ransoms.

M.H. Keen argues that the poor were treated with great brutality. The Church's code, which said that peasants should be protected from the ravages of war, was honoured more often in the breach than the observance.[10] By the time of the knight of the sorrowful countenance, even the knightly ideal was held up to ridicule. The Hundred Year's War ended in 1453. *Don Quixote* by Cervantes (1547-1616), only a century and a half later, looked at the ideals in a comic light. Nevertheless, the rules protecting certain classes of people were firmly stated both in canon law and the chivalric code. Vitoria brought these to the fore, to make the protection of non-combatants from a direct attack a matter of moral principle and grounding this in the even more fundamental moral principle about not killing the innocent.

A puzzling question arises today as to why the major theologians of the 'just war' tradition before Vitoria, Augustine and Aquinas, did not make the immunity of non-combatants from direct attack a formal moral principle. Richard Shelley Hartigan has written that he finds no basis for a theologically supported doctrine of innocent immunity in Augustine, and no instance where Augustine 'recommends that mercy replace justice in dealings with an enemy; when victory is secure and a just peace restored, then it is time enough to be merciful to captives'.[11] My own reading of Augustine bears this out, and it is certainly true that Augustine's theory of war lends itself to harsh practice. For Augustine regarded the fault for which a just war was waged as a breach not only of the social order but of the moral order. A just war was an act of punishment, and those who killed in carrying out this punishment were not to blame.

Hartigan suggests that Augustine did not give proper attention to protecting non-combatants because of his sense of solidarity between the individual and society, and because of his belief that the soul of a person who was truly innocent was in the hands of God and nothing could harm him eternally. Nevertheless, too much must not be read into what Augustine did *not* teach. He was certainly highly sensitive to the horror of wars.

If anyone either endures or thinks of them without
mental pain, his is a more miserable plight still for he
thinks himself happy because he has lost all human
feeling.[12]

Furthermore, Augustine taught that war must be waged with
a correct inner attitude, a right intention. In a letter written to
Boniface about 418 he said:

Even in waging war, cherish the spirit of the peace-
maker that, by conquering those whom you attack, you
may lead them back to the advantages of peace . . . Let
necessity therefore, and not your will, slay the enemy
who fights against you.[13]

Elsewhere he wrote that what is to be blamed in war is:

the desire for harming, the cruelty of avenging, an
unruly and implacable animosity, the rage of rebellion,
the lust of domination and the like — these are the
things which are to be blamed in war.[14]

This passage was later quoted by Aquinas to illustrate the
third condition which must be met for a just war, right
intention. It is certainly true that this emphasis on right inner
intention and corrsponding lack of direct teaching on the
immunity of non-combatants provides nothing in the way of
objective restraints on ruthless people who, fighting what
they judge to be a just war, assume that 'anything goes'.
Nevertheless, that attitude must not be attributed to Augustine himself. The thrust of his teaching is that just wars are
waged out of necessity, and the corresponding truth is that
only what is strictly necessary for victory may be done. *If*
there is a right intention, a sound inner disposition, only what
is strictly necessary *will* be done. The problem, of course, is
that we cannot assume a right inner disposition even in those
fighting in a just cause. Teaching about right intention needs
to be spelt out in terms of who is to be protected and under
what circumstances. This was done by Vitoria.

Whatever was missing in Augustine, Vitoria remedied it. The immunity of non-combatants from direct attack was made a clear moral principle. This principle was strongly affirmed by the next great theologian of the 'just war' tradition, another Spaniard, the Jesuit Fransisco de Suarez (1548-1617). Suarez asserted:

> I hold that innocent persons as such may in nowise be slain, even if the punishment inflicted upon their state would, otherwise, be deemed inadequate; but incidentally they may be slain, when such an act is necessary in order to secure victory.[15]

Suarez then goes on to consider the objections to this view and argues that it is a moral imperative which applies even to states, and it is applicable whatever is said in the Old Testament that implies the contrary.

The teaching of the great Spanish theologians was taken up by Hugo Grotius (1583-1645), generally regarded as the founder of international law. Grotius repeated with great insistence the moral inviolability of non-combatants, listing the classes of people who were to be included. He mentions all the categories put forward by the Canonists and adds 'those who give their labour to honourable literary studies useful to mankind'.[16] Grotius is interesting and important because he writes as a lawyer rather than a moralist (though he is a moralist) and theologian. He is highly aware of what is allowed and forbidden by natural law and by the *ius gentium* or law of nations. But he is no less aware that the gospel ethic should permeate and influence what the natural law and the *ius gentium* allow. His stress is on mercy no less than justice:

> An enemy therefore who considers not what human laws permit, but what is his duty, what is righteous and pious, will spare hostile blood and will never inflict death, except either to avoid death, or evils like death or to crimes which are capital in desert. And even to some who have deserved that, he will remit all, or at least, capital punishment, either out of humanity, or for some other plausible cause.[17]

Again:

> We must hold that if justice do not require, at least
> mercy does, that we should not, except for weighty
> causes, tending to the safety of many, undertake
> anything which may involve innocent persons in
> destruction.[18]

Grotius, in the way he holds together what on the one hand
the natural law and the *ius gentium* permit and on the other
what the Gospel ethic enjoins, has a grasp of that tension
inherent in the New Testament, which has been lost in many
theologians. It was maintained in earlier chapters that there is
an inescapable dualism in the New Testament, which must
not be lost, and that whilst we have to affirm the steps that are
necessary to hold together human society we must all the
time allow these steps to be judged and permeated by the
absolute ideal of the gospel. This tension was kept by
Grotius. As Sydney Bailey has written:

> Grotius does not fail to remind his readers of the
> perfectionism of 'Sermon on the Mount' Christianity.
> For thirteen centuries, this emphasis has been confined
> to a few utopian sects, while the mainstream of
> Christian theology has been more concerned with
> accommodating 'the law of the gospel' to the require-
> ments of the secular world. Yet here was Grotius, a
> Christian and a humanist, a man of the world, a
> professional bureaucrat, formulating a theory of inter-
> national law 'from an entirely secular point of view' and
> yet constantly reiterating the need to love the enemy, to
> give him the benefit of the doubt, to be killed rather
> than to kill.[19]

Since the time of Grotius the prinicple of non-combatant
immunity has become firmly established both in international
law and in the military law of many nations. The detailed
implications of this basic principle have been spelt out in legal
form. One area where there has been legal uncertainty has
been the aerial bombing of cities. Moral concern about this

has, however, remained. In Britain during World War 2, Bishop Bell condemned the allied policy of area bombing. In the United States, Father John Ford SJ did the same. It was Father Ford, too, who first condemned the bombing of Hiroshima and Nagasaki using the criteria of the 'just war' tradition.[20]

As has been shown in this chapter, the principle of non-combatant immunity as a formal moral principle arose surprisingly late in the tradition. First, there came the actual practical steps taken by church assemblies and church lawyers in the ninth and tenth centuries to limit the amount of destruction and suffering caused to peasants, clerics and so on. Then, with Vitoria in the sixteenth century, non-combatants were identified as *innocentes,* the innocent whom Aquinas taught must never be killed directly. From this late development, some have drawn the conclusion that the principle of non-combatant immunity is not an absolute moral principle but simply a rule of thumb or guide as to how to minimize non-combatant casualties.[21] Two points may be made about this erroneous conclusion. First, it confuses two principles. There is the general moral obligation to keep casualties, all casualties, but especially non-combatant casualties down to the absolute minimum. This principle is derived from the fact that a just war is only fought in the first place in order to protect life. It must therefore be fought in a way that expresses and preserves that aim. If war is fought with a wanton disregard for life, the main purpose, the only valid *raison d'être,* is contradicted. So every attempt must be made to minimize damage and suffering. This imperative comes to the fore in the principle of proportion which is considered in a later chapter. This allows for the possibility of a war being so destructive that the evil outweighs the original good for which it was fought. But this obligation, to keep casualties to a minimum, though of crucial importance, is different from the no less important principle that non-combatants must not be directly attacked.

Secondly, it is true that the principle as a formal moral principle, arose relatively late, but so did the moral prohibition of slavery. We would not deny that slavery is at all times and under all circumstances, wrong. So is directly killing non-combatants. It is, simply, murder. The only moral justification for killing anyone in war is that this is an absolute necessity, the enemy can be rendered harmless no other way. But non-combatants are, by definition, no threat. No more are prisoners of war. Killing non-combatants, as Lieutenant Calley did in Vietnam, like killing prisoners of war, as the Japanese did in World War 2, is murder.

Paul Ramsey, for whose ethical position the principle of non-combatant immunity has been central, grounded it in the Christian ethic of love.[22] He argued that when the Church first made the decision to support just wars it was on the basis of love: love leading those in power to protect the innocent who were being attacked and violated. But the same motive which led them to defend the attacked led them also to throw a wall of immunity round the innocent on the other side. Ramsey sought to justify this conclusion historically by contrasting the justification of war in Aquinas, where it is based on the right of self-defence, with that in Augustine; and he claimed to find the origin of the principle in non-combatant immunity in Augustine himself. As stated earlier, the principle is not in Augustine. Nevertheless, Ramsey's Christian reasoning is sound. It can only be on the basis of love that wars are fought, to protect those who are being harmed. That same love offers protection and immunity to all the harmless, whatever side they are on. The purpose of a just war is to protect the harmless. The harmless on the side of the enemy have just as much right to protection as the harmless on one's own side. Killing a harmless person on one's own side without due cause would be murder. Killing a harmless person on the enemy side is no less murder. So it was that Vitoria and Suarez saw no more need for the justification of the principle of non-combatant immunity than that, like all killing of the harmless, it is contrary to the natural law.

Further objections to the status of non-combatant immunity as an immutable principle that have become particularly sharp as a result of the nuclear age will be considered in the next chapter. The point here is that with Vitoria this principle became a central tenet of the 'just war' tradition; and although it was relatively late in terms of the tradition that the principle was formally recognized as such, this tardiness does not effect its validity and authority now that we have acknowledged it. For, as we have seen, it is grounded both in the tenets of natural law and the Christian ethic of love, which seeks to protect the harmless.

Notes

1. *De Indis et de iure belli relections,* 15. English translation by J.P. Bate and E. Nys. Scott's Classics of International Law, NY, 1964. Cited as *De Indis.*
2. *De Indis,* 37.
3. Commentary on the *Summa Theologica* of St Thomas Aquinas. Question 40, Article I, Section II.
4. *De Indis,* 36.
5. *De Indis,* 60.
6. *De Indis,* 38.
7. See George Duby, *The Chivalrous Society,* Arnold, 1977, Chapter 8.
8. See Frederick H. Russell, *The Just War in the Middle Ages,* CUP, 1977.
9. See J.T. Johnson, *Ideology, Reason, and the Limitation of War,* Princeton, 1975, pp.42–75.
10. M.H. Keen, *The Laws of War in the Late Middle Ages,* 1965.
11. Richard Shelley Hartigan, 'Saint Augustine on War and Killing: the Problem of the Innocent', *Journal of Historical Ideas,* April–June 1966, pp.195–204.
12. *Contra Faustum,* Bk XIX, Chapter VII.
13. *Epistle ad Bonifacium,* 189, VI.
14. *Contra Faustum,* Bk.XII, Chapter LXXIV.
15. *De triplici virtute theologica de charitate,* disputation 13, Section 15, English translation by G.L. Williams and A. Brown in *Selections from Three Works by ...Suarez,* Scott's Classics of International Law, NY, 1964. Cited as *De triplici.*
16. Hugo Grotius, *De iure belli ac pacis,* Bk 3, Chapter 11, Section 10. Cited as *De iure.*
17. *De iure,* 3. 11. 7.
18. *De iure,* 3. 11. 8.
19. Sydney D. Bailey, *Prohibitions and Restraints in War,* OUP, 1972, p.35.
20. John Ford, 'The Morality of Obliteration Bombing', first printed in 'Theological Studies' in 1944 and reprinted in *War and Morality*

ed. R. Wasserstrom, Wadsworth, 1970. For an assessement of the morality of this see Barrie Paskins and Michael Dockrill, *The Ethics of War,* Duckworth, 1979, Part 1, and Leonard Cheshire, *The Light of Many Suns,* Methuen, 1985.

21. E.g. William O'Brien, *The Conduct of Just and Limited War,* Praeger, 1981 and his earlier *Nuclear War, Deterrence and Morality,* Newman, 1967.

22. Paul Ramsey, *War and the Christian Conscience,* Duke, 1961, Chapter 3.

CHAPTER EIGHT

Non-combatant immunity and nuclear weapons

The principle of non-combatant immunity, as an immutable moral principle, has come under attack for a number of reasons highlighted by the nuclear age. Some have argued that the distinction between combatant and non-combatant can no longer be made, because modern war is total war. Others have criticized the principle because they think there is no moral distinction between non-combatants who are killed directly and those who die as a result of an attack on a military target. This latter criticism necessitates a consideration of the principle of double effect.

It is often said that the distinction between combatants and non-combatants is no longer valid because modern war is total, engaging all the citizens of a state. It is indeed true that warfare today between the major industrialized nations is very different from what it was in the eighteenth century. As a result of Napoleon's concept of 'the nation in arms', and because of industrialization, war is no longer a kind of ritualized combat between professional forces. But does this mean that the traditional distinction completely fails? Are schoolchildren to be counted as combatants? Ladies in an old people's home? Those in hospital? It is true that a lady in an old person's home might be subjectively more guilty for the prosecution of an unjust war than a reluctant conscript. But the 'just war' tradition does not seek to ascertain subjective guilt. The crucial distinction, as we have seen, is between those who are an objective threat and those who are not. A soldier (or a clergyman) with a machine gun is an objective threat in a way that an old lady, however full of hate, is not. Furthermore, whilst it might be true that in an indirect way very many people support the war effort, even children who send letters of encouragement to fathers at the front and ladies who knit socks, not everyone contributes to the *military* aspect of the war effort. Children would write letters and grannies knit socks anyway. It may be true that the baker has some of his bread eaten by soldiers, but he would be baking bread and they would be eating it, even if they were not soldiers and there was no war. On the other hand, munitions workers, political leaders, and some electronic experts contribute directly to the military aspect of the war. They can clearly be termed combatants in a way that the baker, the greengrocer and the confectioner cannot.[1]

If a war has broken out the prime purpose of the operation is to render the enemy forces incapable of prosecuting the war further, of rendering the aggressor harmless. There is an important qualification of this purpose in the nuclear age. If a nuclear war broke out the prime purpose would not be to incapacitate the enemy's missiles, but to bring the enemy to the negotiating table in order to bring the war to a halt as rapidly as possible. But this point does not affect the definition of a combatant. For this purpose anyone who poses an objective threat, such as a tank commander or bomber pilot and those who support and supply those aspects of their activities that are threatening, count as a combatant. A combatant, in short, is someone actively prosecuting a war or contributing to the military aspect of the war effort.

The principles of non-combatant immunity and proportion (which is considered in a later chapter) are closely related to another principle, that of double effect. This was formulated by Thomas Aquinas (1225-74) in these words:

> A single act may have two effects, of which one alone is intended, whilst the other is incidental to that intention. But the way a moral act is to be classified depends on what is intended, not on what goes beyond such an intention, since this is merely incidental thereto . . . In the light of this distinction we can see that an act of self-defence may have two effects: the saving of one's own life, and the killing of the attacker. Now such an act of self-defence is not illegitimate just because the agent intends to save his own life, because it is natural for anything to want to preserve itself in being as far as

it can. An act that is properly motivated may, nevertheless, become vitiated if it is not proportionate to the end intended. And this is why somebody who uses more violence than is necessary to defend himself will be doing something wrong. On the other hand, the controlled use of counter-violence constitutes legitimate self-defence, for according to the law *it is legitimate to answer force* with force provided it goes no further than due defence requires.[2]

In recent years the principle of double effect has been rejected by some analysts of the 'just war' tradition. It has been argued, for example, that if a munitions factory set in an urban area is bombed with the certain knowledge that a good number of civilians will be killed, these deaths must be counted as equally part of the intention as bombing the factory. If such deaths are clearly *foreseen* they are also *intended,* the argument runs, and it is hypocritical to suggest that they are beside the intention.[3]

The principle of double effect and its related concept of intention raise some of the most fundamental questions of moral philosophy. For example, if a person judges an action to be right or wrong simply on the basis of the consequences that will flow from it, the principle of double effect will have no place. All consequences will be equally intended and the right action will be the one that minimizes the evil and maximizes the good. On the other hand if some actions, such as raping a ten year old child, are regarded as wrong in themselves, whatever the circumstances, and even if beneficial consequences come of them, the principle of double effect is crucial. For according to this view an action, such as bombing a munitions factory, might in itself be right and the killing of civilians in the area, though much regretted, would not be regarded as an immoral act (unless the deaths were disproportionate) because they would not be directly intended. The position assumed here is that acts can be judged right or wrong in themselves and therefore the principle of double effect is still an essential tool of moral analysts.

First, it is possible and important to distinguish intention from motive. A person's motive is an entirely inward matter known in its totality to God and only in part to friends or spiritual advisers.

Secondly, it is possible to have an intention which is a purely inward matter, as when someone says that they intend to write a novel but never actually put pen to paper. Normally, however, the intention of an action is related both to a person's mental processes and to the immediate effects of their action. So, thirdly, two extreme positions must be rejected. One suggests that the intention of an action is to be judged simply on the basis of what is going on in a person's mind. The other says that the intention of the action is to be discerned only from its consequences.

Fourthly, therefore, the immediate effects of an action are an indication of the intention. Although Aquinas, in the passage quoted, could be understood to mean that intention is a purely mental matter — to save one's life — the main thrust of Christian moral theology has denied this. As Father John Ford put it, if a centre of population is about to be devastated by bombs it is specious for the person dropping them 'to let go his bombs and withhold his intention as far as the innocent are concerned'. What the bombs actually do has to be taken as an indication of the intention of the action.

Fifthly, however, as already suggested, consequences alone are not usually enough to indicate intention. In certain extreme cases they do. If a person tries to kill a fly on someone's head by smashing it with a hammer, this might reasonably be taken as a sign that they wanted to kill the person rather than the fly. But even in extreme cases the effects of an action are not necessarily an adequate indicator. In World War 2, Jewish leaders asked the allies to bomb concentration camps, on the grounds that though the inmates would be killed it would save lives in the long run. Few would claim that the intention of such a bombing would be to kill the Jews in them. Or, to take a less tragic example, a person hitting a golf ball on a fairway always manages to cut a divot. Someone from another planet watching their action might deduce that its intention was to ruin the fairway. But, interpreting that golf swing in the light of what is customary, we conclude that the intention is to hit the golf ball. We would distinguish this from the behaviour of someone who insisted on standing a yard from the ball and driving a club an inch into the turf. In that latter instance, we correctly deduce from the circumstances and effects of the action that the intention of the action is to despoil the fairway. But consequences alone are not usually enough to indicate intention.

Sixthly, it is possible and necessary to distinguish between the immediate effects of an action and the longer term consequences. Some effects are necessary to the description of any action. When someone is shot there is a train of effects — messages through the nerves, the flexing of muscles, the pulling of the trigger, the projection of the bullet, the entry of the bullet into the target and so on. It is not informative to restrict the intention to 'squeezing the trigger' or 'releasing the bullet'. We would normally, and correctly, say that the intention was to shoot the person. Whether the intention was to shoot to kill would have to be deduced from other features in the situation. On the other hand, it is equally unhelpful to take into account long term consequences and to say that the intention was to test the skill of the forensic scientist or to improve the profits of the undertaker, all of which are in some sense consequences of pulling the trigger. The intention of an action, therefore, is to be deduced, at least in part, from the immediate effects of an action, which can in most cases be distinguished from the longer term consequences which are not materially significant to the description of the act.

David Fisher in *Morality and the Bomb*[4] maintains that the main moral distinction is between an action which is within our control and one which is not. He argues that if an action is in our control the difference between what is directly intended and what is foreseen but unintended virtually vanishes. It is indeed true that there is a crucial difference between what is in my control, for example, driving a car, and what is outside it, a puncture in the tyre of a car approaching me, and I have a responsibility for the one and not the other. But this is not the only important moral difference. Fisher argues that there is no real distinction between these two circumstances: (1) the agent intended to crush my hand; and (2) the agent foresaw that my hand would inevitably be crushed as the result of what he was doing and was, none the less, willing that it should be crushed. But suppose a baby in the kitchen is just about to tip a saucepan of boiling water over itself. You make a grab for the baby knowing that you are likely to tread on the hand of the person wiping the floor just below the stove. The person whose hand is crushed has no difficulty seeing that the safety of the baby outweighs the pain to his hand (the action was therefore proportionate), and that there is a crucial difference between this pain brought about as a result of a saving action and a hand being deliberately stamped on.

We conclude therefore that the principle of double effect remains a crucial tool of moral analysis. Certain actions are to be judged intrinsically wrong, for example the direct killing of non-combatants. On the other hand, the rightness or wrongness of the foreseen but unintended consequences of an action which is legitimate in itself, e.g. the deaths of civilians brought about from the bombing of a munitions factory, is to be judged by the principle of proportion. A distinction can and must be made between what is intended and what is foreseen but unintended.

The attempt to downgrade the principle of non-combatant immunity from the status of an absolute moral principle has been undertaken for two rather different reasons. First, there are those who maintain that deterrence in the last resort depends upon directly threatening non-combatants. But, though deterrence in the past may have been based on a policy of directly attacking non-combatants, this is no reason why it should in the future. It is argued in Chapters Ten and Eleven, that it is perfectly possible to have a credible policy of nuclear deterrence which does not depend upon the threat, even in the last resort, to attack civilians *qua* civilians. A deterrence policy that avoids direct attacks on civilians *qua* civilians is both a practical possibility and a moral obligation.

The other reason why some wish to stress the obligation to minimize civilian casualties, rather than treating the principle of non-combatant immunity as an absolute, is because of the devastation that would be caused by a nuclear warhead being aimed at a military target near or in a large city. This would cause the most terrible loss of life, but some might want to argue that it was legitimate because it was not a violation of the principle of non-combatant immunity. Whether it would violate the principle of proportion is another matter. This question of proportion is discussed in Chapter Ten.

Clearly there is an overriding obligation to keep casualties down. A targeting policy must be evolved, and weapons systems developed, which can provide a credible deterrence whilst at the same time keeping the prospect of loss of life at much lower levels. To anyone of moral sensitivity this must be a prime moral obligation.

But that does not mean to say that the principle of non-combatant immunity has ceased to be valid in its own right. It remains both valid and of crucial importance, not simply as a guide to how casualties are likely to be minimized but as a moral principle not to be contravened.

For nearly fifteen years after the dropping of atomic bombs on Hiroshima and Nagasaki the moral debate was conducted in somewhat general ethical terms. In England it was not until the publication of *Nuclear Weapons and Christian Conscience* in 1961 that the principle of non-combatant immunity came firmly to the fore. Two essays in particular in that book made their mark, the ones by Elizabeth Anscombe and Walter Stein. Neither writer was a pacifist, indeed Elizabeth Anscombe argued against pacifism in words that have since become famous:

> Now pacifism teaches people to make no distinction between the shedding of innocent blood and the shedding of any human blood. And in this way pacifism has corrupted enormous numbers of people who will not act according to its tenets. They become convinced that a number of things are wicked which are not; hence, seeing no way of avoiding 'wickedness', they set no limits to it.[5]

The main limit that pacifism helps people to ignore, according to Miss Anscombe, is the immunity of non-combatants from direct attack. Both she and Walter Stein argue passionately for the retention of that principle and, on that basis, against the policy of nuclear deterrence as then conceived.

In the United States at that time it was not so much Roman Catholics, whom one might have expected, as a Methodist, Paul Ramsey, who in a remarkable series of articles and essays in the early 1960s put the principle of non-combatant immunity at the centre of his thinking.[6] Unlike Anscombe and Stein, who are nuclear pacifists, Ramsey wanted to defend a policy of nuclear deterrence but he wanted one that did not depend on attacking or threatening to attack non-combatants directly. Some of Ramsey's prose is convoluted but on the whole this reflects not lack of clarity of thought, but an honest and serious attempt to wrestle with the genuinely new moral dilemmas set by the nuclear age.

As a result of Ramsey's work and its increasing influence in the writings of others, the authors of *The Church and the Bomb* (the report of a working party of the Board of Social Responsibility of the General Synod of the Church of England) deliberately reflected on nuclear deterrence using the criteria of the 'just war' tradition (even though some members of the working party were pacifists). It was all the more surprising therefore that the report should have confused and conflated some distinctions so carefully made by Paul Ramsey. For example, discussing the use of tactical nuclear weapons it quotes a UN study in which it was suggested that their use in a populated rural part of central Europe would result in 150,000 immediate civilian casualties and a further 70,000 from fall-out. At the same time the equivalent military casualties would be 30,000 immediately dead and 5,000 who would die later from fall-out. The report concludes from this that:

> Such a use of nuclear weapons amounts to the wholesale and foreseen killing and injuring of non-combatants, which cannot be described as discriminate. Nor does appeal to the principle of double effect offer relief. These deaths are not the accidental or incidental result of lawful military action, but are what one is aiming to do in choosing to fight with this type of weapon.[7]

This conclusion confuses the two principles of non-combatant immunity and proportion. As was argued earlier, to foresee is not the same as to intend. The intention of an action is judged by the thrust and direction of the act itself. If a tactical nuclear weapon was used on a significant military target, for example a large tank formation, and the shock of this resulted in both sides coming together to negotiate a speedy end to the conflict before further escalation took place, 100,000 dead as a result of such use could be judged the least evil of the courses of action available at the time. This judgement might be mistaken but, either way, calculation could take place on the basis of the principle of proportion. The point is that it would still be possible to decide that the attack had been on a *military* target. Even if heavy civilian casualties were foreseen as an inevitable (but unintended) result of the attack on the tank formation, this would not be a violation of the principle of non–combatant immunity. It is facile to suggest that if there are more civilian than military deaths this makes it a direct attack on civilians. The purpose of such an attack would be to cripple the tank offensive and bring the war to a halt, not to kill soldiers as such any more than to kill civilians.

In the United States the influential pastoral letter of the Roman Catholic Bishops, *The Challenge of Peace,* likewise set out to work within the criteria of the 'just war' tradition and had no doubt that principle of non–combatant immunity was fundamental. Twice they quoted the crucial statement of the Second Vatican Council:

> Any act of war aimed indiscriminately at the destruction of entire cities or of extensive areas along with their population is a crime against God and man himself. It merits unequivocal and unhesitating condemnation.[8]

On the basis of this the Bishops asserted:

> Under no circumstances may nuclear weapons or other instruments of mass slaughter be used for the purpose of destroying population centres or other predominantly civilian targets.[9]

Did the American Roman Catholic Bishops judge, however, that every use of nuclear weapons would breach this principle? The letter has been variously interpreted. Some have argued that it forbids on moral grounds every conceivable use of nuclear weapons. That is not my reading. There is no doubt that the whole thrust of the report is against the use of nuclear weapons, and there is extreme scepticism about the possibility of any use meeting the criteria of discrimination and proportion. Nevertheless, there is no unequivocal condemnation: no statement that use in any and every circumstance would be *morally* wrong. This reading is borne out by the verbal evidence given to the US House of Representatives committee on Foreign Affairs by John O'Connor, Archbishop of New York, and Cardinal Bernadin. They were questioned in some detail about the pastoral letter, and the questioner told Cardinal Bernadin that he wanted 'to get down to the bottom line . . . the bottom line is, can you use nuclear weapons?' And he suggested that the pastoral letter had argued for a system of deterrence based on bluff.[10] Cardinal Bernadin strongly denied this and stated that the bishops were arguing for a system of deterrence that kept within the bounds of morality; 'the deterrence is not based on a bluff, but on a willingness to use only those means which would morally be acceptable'. Further pressed, Cardinal Bernadin then said that 'you can't intend to use these weapons against cities'. Furthermore, 'we are very, very sceptical that the use of these weapons could be contained within morally acceptable limits'. Archbishop O'Connor was then asked whether and when such weapons might be used. After stating that a nuclear war cannot be won and must never be fought, the Archbishop did then finally admit that there could in theory be situations in which the principles of discrimination and proportion could be met:

> I think it is conceivable in a naval engagement at sea, tactical nuclear weapons could be used and it is conceivable that if one could separate the industrial complex, or the purely military force at hand from civilian populations, it is conceivable that a tactical nuclear weapon, if it could be guaranteed that it could be that controllable, that it could be used.

This, perhaps, should have been said a great deal earlier. It is obvious that, for example, the use of a tactical nuclear weapon on a fleet at sea does not violate the principle of non-combatant immunity in the way that the My Lai massacre did, or, in some people's judgement, did the allied bombing of Dresden. It can only help the honesty and clarity of the debate to agree that there are in theory, at least, some circumstances in which the use of nuclear weapons would not constitute a direct attack on non-combatants (and this is conceded by some opponents of deterrence). But this is only theory. What about the reality? Walter Stein presses the point:

> Then there is that 'fleet at sea' . . . one has to admit, 'a certain type of nuclear bomb' *could* be used against it . . . whilst remaining discriminate in its effects; though this still leaves the question how many of these fleets, or armies concentrating in deserts perhaps, are likely to be about? What we do on the other hand know with some directness is that many hundreds or thousands of 'a certain type of bomb', and many thousands or ten-thousands of bombs of other types (not necessarily negligible) are accumulating in various parts of the globe . . . And we do know that American civil defence specialists have found it convenient to give a new word — a unit — to our language: 'megacorpse': one million dead bodies . . .[11]

The fact that there are even a few uses of nuclear weapons that would not inevitably violate the principle of non-combatant immunity, however, is crucial for the morality of deterrence, a point that is considered further in the chapter dealing with deterrence. Nevertheless, Stein's point is one that needs to be faced. To think only of a possible use on a fleet at sea or an army in the desert is wilful make-believe. Public conscious-ness, to put it no higher, is of nuclear weapons being used on cities and of massive civilian casualties. There are, however, two ways in which such a terrible scenario could come about. First, it is possible that nuclear weapons are already targeted on cities. Secondly there is the fear that even if they are not so targeted now, any small scale use of nuclear weapons would rapidly escalate to the point where they were. The point about escalation which is of vital significance, is considered in the next chapter, for it affects the principles of discrimination and proportion equally. The first point, about present targeting, is considered here.

A discussion of targeting raises three main questions. First, what is necessary in order to deter a potential enemy? Secondly, what is present targeting policy? Thirdly, what are the practical implications of the principle of non-combatant immunity? The first question is considered more fully in the chapter on deterrence. Here only the conclusion is stated, that effective deterrence does not depend on counter-population policies. The second question is difficult to answer because of the secrecy which inevitably surrounds such a subject. All we have on record, from the British Government's 1980 *Open Government Document on Trident* (OGD 80/23), is that targets are 'key aspects of Soviet state power'. This could include everything from the Kremlin itself to a missile base in remotest Siberia. As stated the formula meets the formal requirements of the principle of non-combatant immunity, for 'key aspects of Soviet state power' clearly means political and military targets. What it does not do is to indicate whether those targets are in or close to centres of population. As was shown in the previous chapter the principle of non-combatant immunity was preceded by the practical steps taken by churchmen in the tenth and eleventh centuries to limit the harm done to non-combatants in war. In other words there is also the more general moral requirement to keep the destruction of innocent life to the minimum. It would be possible to apply the principle of non-combatant immunity in a legalistic way that completely missed the other basic moral imperative if, for example, it was argued that an attack on the Kremlin was justified because it is the prime political target. Here the two principles of discrimination and proportion tend to converge in that both are related to the moral imperative to keep loss of life to a minimum. So, although 'key aspects of Soviet state power' meets the formal requirements of a moral targeting policy, it does not satisfy the basic moral common sense of ordinary people who ask if those targets are set in or near cities.

The third question concerns the practical implications of the principle of discrimination. For, even if it was held that present targeting policy could not be justified on moral grounds, it could still be argued that a policy of nuclear deterrence would be moral if the targets were different. Deterrence is not an impersonal 'thing' any more than weapons are things with an autonomous life. Both are products of human minds and can be used in various ways in accord with human choices. Paul Ramsey argued that we can and must have a targeting policy that is moral. More recently James Turner Johnson has argued the same point.[12] Johnson, an accomplished historian of the 'just war' tradition, has tried to apply his historical insights to the contemporary scene. He concludes that 'reasonable options exist to take us away from counter-population targeting toward a more morally defensible policy'. He urges a shift away from the kind of thinking that has been in evidence since the second World War, that war must be prosecuted to the limit of one's capacity; and the development of new weapons, as well as strategies, politics and tactics 'in the service of a morally informed intentionality'. Unfortunately, when Johnson begins to suggest what these might be, he becomes unconvincing. He recommends a decapitation policy, that is, targeting the military and political leadership of the enemy. But paradoxically (and sadly) it is a crucial factor in bringing wars to an end that enough enemy political leadership has to be left intact in order to negotiate an end to the conflict. Political leadership with the authority to stop the war has to be left in being. Johnson also suggests the development of weapons to be used against satellites (ASATS). This might seem an attractive idea, for satellites are a long way away from human beings: but military satellites now play a crucial role in the stability of deterrence. They enable the super-powers to know where the other side's missiles are placed and to see very quickly if any are released. Further, they enable them to feel confident they could control their forces in the event of a war. These are weighty factors in resisting any temptation to strike first. It is also quite unclear how the destruction of the enemy's satellites could constitute a penalty so severe that the prospect of it would offer high assurance of successful deterrence.

Although Johnson's practical proposals lack conviction, the moral imperative behind them has validity. Deterrence can only be moral if it is based on a targeting that is moral. This certainly means keeping nuclear weapons away from centres of civilian population. What it might include is explored further in the chapter on deterrence, when the question of what is necessary to deter is considered.

Notes

1. A good statement of the reasons for the distinction, in secular terms, is given by Michael Walzer, *Just and Unjust Wars*, Penguin, 1978.
2. *Summa Theologica*, II/III, Question 64, Article 7.
3. The fiercest critique of the principle of double effect applied to war is still that of Robert E. Osgood and Robert W. Tucker, *Force, Order, Justice*, John S. Hopkins, 1967, p.310–12. Their view is shared by William V. O'Brien, *The Conduct of Just and Limited War*, Praeger, NY, 1981, pp.46–7. David Fisher, *Morality and the Bomb*, Croom Helm, 1985, pp.30–41 and Barrie Paskins and Michael Dockrill, *The Ethics of War*, Duckworth, 1979, pp.230–33 are also critical. Elizabeth Anscombe has argued in favour, *War and Murder* in War and Morality, p.50, as has Paul Ramsey, *The Just War*, Charles Scribner's, 1968, pp.398–424.
4. *Morality and the Bomb*, Chapter 3.
5. 'War and Murder' in *Nuclear Weapons and Christian Conscience*, ed. Walter Stein, Merlin Press, 1961, p.56.
6. Paul Ramsey, *The Just War*, Scribner's, NY, 1968. An assessment of Ramsey's contribution is made in Edward Laarman, *Nuclear Pacifism, 'Just War' thinking today*, Lang, NY, 1984.
7. The Church of England Board of Social Responsibility, *The Church and the bomb*, Hodder and Stoughton, 1982, p.127.
8. Vatican II, *The Pastoral Constitution on the Church in the Modern World*, 80.
9. *The Challenge of Peace*, CTS/SPCK, 1983, p.147.
10. Statement on 26 June 1984 to the US House of Representatives, Committee on Foreign Affairs, 98th Congress, Second Session. In *The Role of Arms Control in US Defence Policy*, pp.172–74.
11. *Nuclear Weapons and Christian Conscience*, p.35.
12. J. T. Johnson, *Can Modern War be Just?* Yale, 1984, pp.148–49.

CHAPTER NINE

The principle of proportion: its development and validity

When people see films depicting the destruction of a city by a nuclear bomb, their instinctive reaction is likely to be: 'This is so terrible, nothing could justify it'. In making that assessment we are judging in accordance with the principle of proportion. For the principle of proportion is a technical phrase for a way of thinking which is familiar to us all. In relation to the destruction of a city by a nuclear device we are in effect saying, 'that evil is *out of proportion* to any possible good'.

Within the Christian tradition the principle of proportion has its origin in four features of the thought of St Thomas Aquinas, though it was only with Francisco de Vitoria that it was applied systematically to the problem of war. First, there was for Aquinas the condition that in order for a war to be just there must be a right intention, that is, those who fight must 'intend the advancement of good, or the avoidance of evil'.[1] In Augustine and probably in Aquinas himself, this intention is primarily a matter of personal motivation, of having the right inner disposition. But it is a criterion that lends itself to rational application in terms of the consequences of going to war or refraining from doing so. Secondly, as we have seen, in his teaching on private self-defence Aquinas taught that whilst this was lawful it could be rendered unlawful if the defendent used 'more than necessary violence'.[2] In such a case the act of self-defence was 'out of proportion to the end', and Aquinas refers to 'the jurists' in support of this opinion. Thirdly, in his teaching on sedition Aquinas taught that the attempt to overthrow a tyranny did not count as sedition, 'unless indeed the tyrant's rule be disturbed so inordinately that his subjects suffer greater harm from the consequent disturbance than from the tyrant's government'.[3] In other words, those suffering oppression are to consider the likely outcome of trying to throw it off. For an attempt at revolution could lead to even greater suffering than is already having to be endured, in which case, although there might be a just cause to rebel, this would be outweighed by an application of the principle of proportion. Fourthly, there is the general teaching of Aquinas on prudence as a virtue which, following Aristotle, Aquinas rated very highly, particularly in those who had responsibility for public affairs, such as politicians and soldiers. When considering the effects of some legitimate action, a person might conclude that the unintended but foreseen consequences would outweigh the good of that which was intended. Hence the need in moral decision making for foresight and circumspection, particularly amongst those who have responsibility for the common good.

Three centuries later Francisco de Vitoria doubted very much whether the frequent wars in Europe were in the interest of the people as a whole, but it was what the Spanish were doing in South America that particularly appalled him. In a letter of 1534, he wrote of events in the Indies, 'at the mention of which my blood runs cold'. As was seen in Chapter Seven, it is to Vitoria that we owe the formulation of the principle of non-combatant immunity, but it was the question of proportion that concerned him even more, so that it became almost an obsession. Vitoria argued that great attention must be paid to the fact that, though a war might be lawful in itself, it could become unlawful through 'some collateral circumstances'. War should be waged for the common good. So:

> If one city cannot be recaptured without greater evil befalling the state, such as the devastation of many cities, great slaughter of human beings, provocation of princes, occasions for new wars to the destruction of the Church (in that an opportunity is given to pagans to invade and seize the lands of Christians), it is indubitable that the prince is bound rather to give up his own rights and abstain from war.[4]

If, for example, the King of France had a right to retake Milan but as a result both France and Milan would suffer intolerable ills, it would not be right for him to retake it. It is clear from this and other passages that Vitoria has foremost in his mind human suffering and destruction of property, but he also considers the good of the Church as a whole. It is also to be noted that he takes into account the suffering afflicted on the enemy, as well as that suffered by one's own side. Further, though he is primarily concerned with immediate ills, he also includes remoter consequences such as 'occasions for new wars'. Another passage makes it clear that the universal good has to be taken into account, not simply the good of one state or another.

> Since one nation is part of the whole world, and since the Christian province is a part of the whole Christian State, if any war should be advantageous to one province or nation but injurious to the world or to Christendom, it is my belief, that, for this very reason, that war is unjust.[5]

As outlined in Chapter Six, 'just war' theory has two distinct categories, *ius ad bellum* and *ius in bello*. The former concerns the criteria which must be met before the war is fought. The two categories are distinct and should not be confused. For example, it is possible to have a just cause, as was the Allied cause in World War 2, but at the same time it might be judged that some of the means with which the war was prosecuted, for example the bombing of Dresden, offended the criteria of *ius in bello*. The principle of proportion applies to both categories. The war as a whole must be judged to be less evil than refraining from war. Further, particular actions within the war must take into account the necessity of proportion. In other words, it would not be right to destroy a whole town, if the enemy headquarters could be pinpointed more precisely and it could be destroyed by an attack resulting in less loss of life. Clearly, however, as Vitoria makes clear, the amount of destruction that is regarded as tragically necessary will depend on the strategic importance of the target. Proportion is a relationship of two factors, not

just one. The capture of a fortress guarding a mountain pass
which is essential for the winning of the war, can 'justify'
significantly larger casualties than an undefended village on
the way. As Vitoria put it:

> If little effect upon the ultimate issue of the war is to be
> expected from the storming of a fortress or a fortified
> town wherein are many innocent folk, it would not be
> right, for the purpose of assailing a few guilty, to slay
> the many innocent by use of fire or engines of war or
> other means likely to overwhelm indifferently both
> innocent and guilty.[6]

Another important point emerges from this passage.
Protecting the innocent from the *indirect* effects of an attack on
a military target is a high priority. It is not only that
non-combatants should not be directly attacked; their protection from suffering and death by whatever means is to be
given very high priority. Vitoria does not spell out the reason
for this, but it is obvious enough: just wars are fought to
protect the innocent. They must therefore be fought in such a
manner as expresses and preserves their purpose. Every hurt
to someone not directly contributing to hostilities raises a
question mark against the reason for which the war was
fought in the first place.

No doubt the stress that Vitoria laid on considering the
consequences of a political or military act reflected in part the
Renaissance mentality. For there had been a growing mood
that people should act less on the basis of heroic notions and
impractical ideals, and more on solid, practical reasons of
state. Machiavelli, who was only eleven years older than
Vitoria, had taught the lessons of statecraft in the most
practical and realistic way, urging the interest of the state as
the governing principle. Vitoria was a Renaissance realist in
urging that the cost must always be counted. Where he
differed from Machiavelli was in stressing that it was the cost
to the adversary and the cost to Christendom that must also
be taken into account; the innocent life, of whatever nation,
had to be valued.

It was perhaps part of this changing attitude to life that

resulted in the idea of war as a punishment receiving less emphasis in Vitoria. If the object of war is primarily to punish the enemy for the wrong he has done, then you have a moral principle which lets you sit fairly light to the consequences of so acting. Even then the punishment must fit the crime, as Vitoria argued:

> It is not lawful for slight wrongs to pursue the authors of the wrongs with war, seeing that the degree of the punishment ought to correspond to the measure of the offence.[7]

But war as punishment was not uppermost in Vitoria's mind, not least because he thought that there could be many people who were subjectively innocent fighting on the other side. Vitoria gave four reasons for going to war; defence, recovery, to avenge a wrong and to secure peace and security. Vitoria stressed that wars ought to be waged for the common good and for that alone. A very careful assessment was therefore needed to ensure that any proposed military action would really be in the general interest.

Suarez considered the necessary conditions for a just war under three headings. The war must be waged by legitimate authority, 'the cause itself and the reason must be just', and 'thirdly, the method of its conduct must be proper, and due proportion must be observed at its beginning, during its prosecution and after victory'.[8] This third condition refers specifically to proportion, but his discussion of just cause also brings it into account. For Suarez argued that it was possible to have a cause which was not unjust in itself but which was a sin against charity. For example, if an otherwise just war would result in a weakening of the Church, it would be a sin against charity. Likewise, if it resulted in great loss to the state against which the war was fought. If the war resulted in disproportionate loss to the state which was prosecuting the war, then this was a sin not only against charity but against justice. Suarez distinguishes the two by stating that, in the case of a sin against justice, restitution has to be made to the offended party: in the case of a sin against charity, there is no such obligation to make restitution. The distinction that

Suarez makes between justice and charity may not be entirely satisfactory but in his own way he is making a point made, in Chapter Two, in the discussion on how the absolute ethic of the Christian faith bears upon political and economic life. There it was suggested that political realities have to be recognized, but that these stand under the norm of perfect love towards which we are beckoned to approximate so far as we can, whilst at the same time taking those realities into account. Suarez allows that the good of the Church as a whole (by which he meant Christian civilization) and the good of the enemy state, should be taken into account and allowed in some instances to override the 'rights' of another state. In the case of a state with a just cause, he says that there are 'numerous considerations which may oblige a prince to abandon his right to make war, lest his realm suffer loss'.[9]

Suarez also has a thorough discussion on the degree of certainty of victory that is necessary for the war to be called just. Although this has sometimes been stated as a separate principle, it is in fact an extension of the principle of proportion. For, if victory is highly unlikely, this would lead to disproportionate loss. This consideration is an important one and it is discussed in Chapter Eleven.

According to Article 51 of the Charter of the United Nations there is only one just cause for war and that is self-defence. Writers in the 'just war' tradition, however, allowed for the possibilities of just wars of offence as well as defence. From the fourteenth century, three distinct causes for a just war were referred to: defence, recovery and punishment. Recovery was subdivided by some writers into the recovery which was a more or less instantaneous upshot of a previous conflict, and recovery after an interval of time. The question arises whether the principle of proportion appplies equally to wars of offence for recovery and punishment and to wars of defence. But, first, a distinction has to be made between a proportion of effectiveness and a proportion of value. The proportion of effectiveness assumes self-defence as a basic right, and then insists that the defence must not go beyond what is necessary to the defence, as in the earlier quotation from Aquinas. If someone attacks you with a cushion and you proceed to batter him to death, this is out of proportion, it goes beyond what is necessary. All writers in the 'just war' tradition from Aquinas onwards insist on this point. But the proportion of value raises a further question: whether the war should not be waged at all because of the great loss that might ensue. Vitoria and Suarez are in no doubt that many otherwise just wars of recovery and punishment ought not to be fought, because of this consideration. But what about wars of defence? Should they be fought even if the prospect of victory is slight and the probability of disproportionate suffering high? Both Vitoria and Suarez treat wars of defence differently from wars of offence. Vitoria firmly rejects the view that in a defensive war we ought to flee rather than fight. Otherwise 'wrongdoers would become readier and bolder for wrongdoing', for they could do wrong with impunity. Suarez, in his discussion on the likelihood of victory, argues that if the chance of victory is less than the chance of defeat in an offensive war in almost every case that war should be avoided. But 'if the war is defensive, it should be attempted; for in that case it is a matter of necessity'.[10]

Although these writers made a distinction between wars of defence and wars of offence and took the right of self-defence for granted, there are reasons today for applying the proportion of value to defensive wars as well as offensive ones. First, on certain principles of these writers themselves, it would so apply. Suarez has an interesting discussion on whether, instead of a major conflict, each side could pick a small force and resolve the quarrel by a kind of duel. He argues that this is morally permissible and indeed desirable, for it would reduce the suffering and loss to both sides. Suarez then considers the objection that a prince who undertakes this kind of duel is binding himself to refrain from protecting those whom he has an obligation to protect. Suarez comments:

> The duty of defending the innocent is a precept that binds, not without intermission, but only when it can advantageously be carried out.[11]

It is therefore legitimate to substitute this kind of duel between small hand-picked forces for a more general war, even though it means refraining from protecting the innocent with the full force of arms,

> under circumstances that to the prudent mind may render the defence of the innocent impossible, for the reason that it would clearly involve grave and general disadvantage.

Both defensive and offensive wars are fought to protect the innocent. If they cannot do that effectively, then even the right to wage a defensive war may have to be waived.

A second reason why the principle of proportion should apply to wars of defence is that, because of Article 51 of the UN Charter, all wars are now likely to be justified as some form of self-defence. It is widely recognized that Article 51 has its limitations, for taken literally it would mean that a state had to wait until it was physically attacked before mounting a defence, whereas if they had taken earlier action it might have averted the worst. Nevertheless, we have the article and as long as we do so nations will seek to justify their actions in terms of it. It is therefore important that the principle of proportion be brought to bear upon these justifications. In terms of the old terminology, the action by the British over the Falkland Islands might have been justified as a war of immediate recovery. In the forum of the UN it had to be seen as a war of self-defence. Whatever the terminology, it is obviously important that the principle of proportion be brought to bear on all possible wars, and there should not be a vast category of 'defensive' wars which are regarded as exempt from this principle.

Then, finally, there is a more philosophical consideration. To make defensive wars exempt from the application of the principle of proportion would in effect make the defence of the state an absolute. It would imply that the state must be defended at whatever the cost. There is an important sense in which the state is the precondition of certain values, particularly democratic values, and it may have to be defended at very great cost. But to say that the state may have to be defended at any cost is to make it an absolute: and this is theologically erroneous. Only God is absolute, and nothing human, not even certain of our most sacred principles, have absolute status. We have to allow for the possibility that in certain circumstances other factors might override them. Although Martin Luther did not consciously adhere to the 'just war' tradition, most of his thinking about war uses its principles. He regarded even defensive wars as subject to other considerations:

> If we are not going to make an adequate, honest resistance that will have some reserve power, it would be far better not to begin a war, but to yield lands and people to the Turk in time, without useless bloodshed, rather than have him win anyhow in an easy battle with shameful bloodshed.[12]

The principle of proportion is open to the criticism that it is such an elastic concept it offers no restraint on what is permissible. This criticism has been powerfully made by Professor Tucker.[13] He considers the principle of proportion under the two heads indicated earlier in this chapter, a proportion of effectiveness and a proportion of value. Taking the proportion of effectiveness to mean that 'acts in self-defence may not be disproportionate to the danger threatened', he suggests this can mean repelling the immediate danger or removing it for all time. For example, if a nation is attacked a proportionate defence might be to halt the advancing troop formations or it might mean destroying command posts, supply depots and munitions factories. Even if defence is limited to repelling the invader the question arises, how far further enemy attempts to attack should be taken into account and allowed for? These are proper questions and there are real difficulties. But as Professor William O'Brien has remarked:

> The function of just-war analysis is to guide the conscience of the individual or society that is looking for moral guidance. If the individual or society is inclined to cheat and to seek spurious justifications, no principles or prescriptions will be safe from abuse. The problem is not with the principle of proportion or with the

principle of discrimination. The problem of abuse will remain the problem of dishonest or hypocritical individuals or nations that misuse these principles.[14]

It is in fact possible to see what constitutes a proportionate defence in some circumstances. For example, if someone is always trying to trip me up on the stairs, it would be a disproportionate response to batter him to death. On the other hand, simply avoiding an outstretched leg is not the only other alternative. Giving the leg a kick or the owner of the leg a push to make him desist from such behaviour is not disproportionate. It was not unreasonable that the Americans should have wanted Soviet missiles completely removed from Cuba. It would have been disproportionate if they had tried to eliminate every Soviet missile threat. There are many blurred edges but this does not obviate the possibility of and necessity of making a judgement.

Underlying the moral and legal requirement for a proportionate defence are some fundamental theological assumptions. First, conflict, struggle and threats are a constant feature of human existence. Any attempt to completely remove all threats to one's security, or any 'war to end all war' is based on an illusion. Secondly, attempts to completely eliminate a danger, by removing it once and for all, are expressions of a hubris which totally identifies the good with one side and the evil with the other. It is another expression of the crusade mentality, the idea of fighting on God's side against God's enemies who must be destroyed. This outlook is alien to the 'just war' tradition, which is based on the premiss that the choices are between sides, all of which are flawed. Because one is more flawed than another, armed resistance may be a tragic necessity but it is not righteous. This resistance aims to prevent the aggressor going on, either through loss of will or loss of ability. It does not seek to eliminate the danger for all time or to destroy the aggressor. The idea of a defence which is proportionate to the threat springs from this underlying theological perspective.

Tucker is even more critical of the proportion of value which he says is 'devoid entirely of the element of specificity'. It is 'implicit in almost every conceivable justification of force' and 'is compatible with almost every justification — or condemnation — of force men have ever given'. Finally, 'it illustrates that a prescription the converse of which is manifestly absurd can tell us very little that is meaningful about how men ought to behave'. The general point made by O'Brien applies here, though once again there are real difficulties to be faced. It is not true, however, that the converse of the principle of proportion is absurd. The converse might be stated as an 'Act irrespective of the consequences'. This is a possible view, a heroic view, but one which, however appealing, stands in contrast to the 'just war' view. There is also a fundamental theological point at stake here. As already stated, nothing of this world, not even the state, has absolute value. There may be extreme circumstances in which the obligation to defend that state may be overridden by a superior moral claim. Finally, the principle of proportion is a reminder that assessing the consequences of possible courses of action and weighing them in the light of fundamental values is a crucial part of Christian decision making. People have sometime fostered the picture of, on the one hand, secular utilitarians counting the cost and, on the other, firm-lipped Christians acting on principles. The 'just war' tradition is a reminder that this is an absurd caricature. Counting the cost is an essential aspect, if not the only aspect, of Christian decision making. Nevertheless, the criticism of lack of specificity remains. How *are* we to weigh one value against another? What scales are there to enable us to put loss of life on one side and cherished principles like liberty on the other?

Grotius laid great stress on the necessity for both a proportion of effectiveness and a proportion of value. Like Suarez he distinguished between the claims of justice and of charity. A ruler has a prime duty to his own people and, if he finds himself with inferior forces, it is his duty to sue for peace. But a Christian is also motivated by charity, and Grotius invests his notion of charity with a specifically Christian content. Because Christ died for us, we ought to give up our rights if seeking them would bring about hurt to other people. It is another example of the way Grotius, like Suarez, preserves the tension inherent in an ethic derived from the New Testament. Grotius was not a pacifist and he was clear that Christ did not teach pacifism. But he knew that duties necessitated by a fallen world have to be permeated by considerations of charity. He was also aware that in decisions concerning war there is usually a clash between the values of liberty and peace. He disagreed with the opinion that it is always better to die rather than submit to the rule of others, 'for life, which is the foundation of all temporal and the occasion of eternal good, is of more value than liberty; whether you take the alternative in a single man or in a people'.[15] He went on to argue that the destruction of a people is the greatest of evils and that when a ship is caught in a storm we throw away the cargo not the passengers.

It is possible to admire the way Grotius seeks to apply the Christian faith to international relations, without agreeing with all his conclusions. His conclusion here, that life is always to be preferred to liberty, does not seem sustainable.[16] There are certain moral values which are fundamental to human community and so therefore to the existence of human personality. For example, the value of truth-telling. Human communities work on the assumption that most people most of the time are telling the truth. Without this assumption, it would not be possible to communicate and there would be neither society nor human beings. Of course human beings lie a great deal, but we still work on the assumption that the truth is being told most of the time. The justification for refusing to tell a lie in a particular instance therefore is not simply the immediate consequences of lying. After all, you might be absolutely certain that you would not be found out and that your lie could not therefore be a bad example, leading others to lie. The justification for truth-telling is that in counting oneself a human being, one is counting oneself part of human society and, in doing that, one is committing oneself to those values without which there can be no society. So that, to stay with the same example, whatever the advantages or disadvantages of telling a lie under certain circumstances, there is a *prima facie* obligation to tell the truth which is independent of any of those consequences. The obligation to resist wrongdoing is a similar kind to this obligation to tell the truth. For if wrongdoers were allowed to do what they wanted, there could be no human society, only continual chaos and anarchy, and in the end the demise of personhood. There is, therefore, a *prima facie* obligation to resist aggression, whether within a society or from outside it, whose justification is not simply the fact that resisting at that moment will bring about less harmful consequences than not resisting. *There is a primary obligation to resist,* whose justification is prior to a consideration of the immediate consequences of resisting or not.

Applying the principle of proportion, therefore, is not simply a matter of weighing up which is the least evil set of consequences. There is a basic obligation to resist and a right to self-defence (which is a collective right rather than an individual right). The principle obliges us to ask whether the circumstances are such that, in this instance, this duty should not be obeyed and this right not exercised. For the point of the principle of proportion is that there may be certain extreme circumstances in which the consequences of resistance would be so horrendous that the obligation to resist is overridden. For extreme situations occur in which other considerations and values take priority over some of our most weighty principles. For example, a person has committed himself to a religious community, and part of the obligation this entails is to attend the daily offices. On the way to church a monk comes across someone who is ill who needs urgent medical attention. Obviously the need of the sick person overrides the prior obligation to join the monks in choir. So sometimes we might have to tell a lie, say, to save someone's life. How horrendous do the consequences have to be for the duty to resist to be overriden? Whatever the difficulties about reaching any precision on this matter one point is quite clear, we *do* reach judgements on this question, ones which are widely shared. For example, most people would agree that NATO was right not to intervene in Hungary in 1956 or in Czechoslovakia in 1968, because of the risk that this would trigger off a war involving nuclear weapons. We accept that the real risk of a major nuclear exchange is an evil that outweighs even the obligation to resist aggression and protect the innocent. It could be argued that an intervention by

NATO would have been a war of offence (in the 'just war' sense) rather than strictly a war of defence. Even so the point holds. *If* it was certain (it is not certain, as will be argued later, but if it was certain) that resistance to a Soviet attack on NATO territory would lead to an all-out nuclear exchange resulting in the total destruction of European society, most people would judge that such an exchange would be the worst possible evil they could imagine and, *if* it was certain, its prospect would override any obligation to resist.

It is important to note what the principle of proportion is not concerned to do, as well as what it is. It is not there to suggest that, if only the positive good is great enough, this will justify any evils in the attainment of that goal. There are those, for example, who posit one or more versions of a perfect society and suggest that, in the light of this, any means to achieve it will be justified. This is ruled out by the Christian ethic. Nor is the principle of proportion simply concerned to evaluate consequences in the light of two values, both of which are held to be equally important, the value of life and the value of liberty. A fundamental assumption in the use of the principle of proportion is that resistance to evil is a duty (for the reasons indicated earlier). Only on the basis of that duty does the principle of proportion come into its own by positing the possibility that the consequences of resisting evil by force might be so horrendous that this *prima facie* duty would have to be given up. What has to be taken into account in considering whether armed resistance would be disproportionate?

First, terrible though it seems, numbers do matter. Any political decision, for example the use of NHS resources, means that some live and some die. How many will die is an important factor in the decision making. Some people will die whatever decision is made, for there is no society with infinite resources. What applies to political decisions is even more true of military ones. Some will die, whatever decisions are made. And the number who will suffer or be destroyed is an important factor in any decision that is made. Secondly, the deaths that are likely to result if military action is *not* taken have to be taken into consideration. It was appalling that the Soviet Union lost 20 million dead in World War 2. But many millions would have died anyway, if they had surrendered to the Nazis and allowed them to carry out their purposes. There was no military resistance to Stalin, and between 15 and 20 million died in his purges according to the latest estimates.

Thirdly, we have to take into account the nature of the threat with which we are faced. Proportion involves a relationship between two terms. One term is provided by the horrific effects of modern weapons. What is the other term? If this is the threat of totalitarianism in one form or another, one which would not be reversible in the short or medium term, this is a weighty factor. There are two dangers here to be avoided. There is the danger of attributing untold evil to the other side in order to cement the internal unity of a state or strengthen a war effort. This danger has its roots in the political processes of all states, which tend to develop external 'enemies', but also in the potential for a 'crusading mentality' to which human beings are prone and to which reference was made earlier. The other danger is to think that one society is as good as another, that there are no significant moral choices to be made, and that there is nothing great enough at stake in human life to fight against or seek to defend. Whilst guarding against both these dangers it is possible to say that societies may be faced with real threats both to their existence and to all they stand for. Not all modern Christian thinking, in its desire to make peace, has taken this possibility seriously.

Fourthly, human values and human life are integrally bound up. It has been suggested that the principle of proportion involves trying to weigh items that are basically incommensurable, values like liberty on the one hand and human suffering on the other. But this is not so. The bodies that lie dead are not just carcases, they are dead human beings, that is, beings for whom moral and spiritual values were an essential aspect of their existance. To be human is to be more than physical. So in cherishing and trying to protect a particular society and way of life, in which certain values are expressed and institutionalized, we are defending *human* life. Better to be Socrates dissatisfied than a pig satisfied. That is why a predicted 'body-count' can never be adequate by itself.

Another way of stating the case is that justice and peace are related to one another, as are justice and order. The only peace worth having is a just peace. The only order that will survive is a just order. In situations of human conflict justice and peace are often in tension and we may have to choose between them in the short term. But essentially they belong together.[17] If a just war is fought it will be for a better order as well as for a more equitable justice.

Human life and human values belong together: they can be weighed on the same scales. This does not, of itself, give any detailed guidance as to how, on any particular issue, a decision is to be made. But it does urge that moral decisions involving both values and loss of human life can and ought to be made.

Notes

1. *Summa Theologica,* II/II Question 40, Article 1.
2. Chapter Eight.
3. *Summa Theologica,* II/II, Question 42, Article 2.
4. *De Indis,* 33.
5. *De Protestate Civile,* 13, a translation is given in an appendix to the book, already cited, in which *De Indis* is translated.
6. *De Indis,* 37.
7. *De Indis,* 48.
8. *De triplici,* disputation 13, 1, 7.
9. *De triplici,* 13, 4, 9.
10. *De triplici,* 13, 4, 10.
11. *De triplici,* 13, 9, 9.
12. 'On War against the Turk', *Luther's Works,* Philadelphia and St Louis, 1953, Volume 46.
13. *Force, Order and Justice,* pp.233–34.
14. *The Conduct of Just and Limited War,* p.339.
15. *De iure belli ac pacis,* 2, 24, 6, 2.
16. An interesting argument why it might be morally proper to resist, even if death is nearly certain, is put forward by Dockrill and Paskins in *The Ethics of War.* They argue for 'the moral significance of the last flutter of humanity in resistance to an oppressor', p.181.
17. See David Hollenbach, SJ, *Nuclear Ethics,* Paulist Press, 1983, Chapter 2.

CHAPTER TEN

Proportion, escalation and nuclear weapons

The previous chapter showed that, though there is a basic right to resist agression there may arise certain circumstances in which, morally, this right is overruled. The evils unleashed by even a just defence might be disproportionate to any possible good achieved by such a defence. If such a prospect seemed likely, it would become a moral obligation to submit. In recent years it has been widely assumed that any possible use of nuclear weapons would indeed be disproportionate. The destruction would be so terrible that nothing, not even a defence of democratic values or a cherished way of life, could justify their use. What truth is there in this widely shared assumption? But, first, a preliminary point.

As stated earlier, the principle of proportion applies both to *ius ad bellum* and *ius in bello,* that is, it is applicable both in considering whether or not the war itself is just and also to the means whereby the war is fought. However, where nuclear weapons are concerned, it is difficult to avoid the conclusion that the two applications contract into one. This is both because the time-scale is likely to be so short, and also because, if nuclear weapons were once used, the target would be chosen not to win a military victory but only for intra-war deterrence, that is, convincing the enemy that he had miscalculated in the first place in going to war. In a war involving only conventional weapons, a judgement can be made that the capture of a particular military stronghold is necessary for achieving victory or that a particular village is not. This is a decision that can be made in relative isolation from overall war aims. If nuclear weapons become a serious prospect, however, their use would be related not to over-coming a particular enemy stronghold but to the overall strategy: convincing the enemy that he had miscalculated and persuading him to bring the war to an end. Would the use of nuclear weapons inevitably be disproportionate? First, an all-out nuclear exchange would in the judgement of most people be an evil that nothing could justify. But, as discussed later, an effective deterrence policy does not depend on such a prospect. All that is necessary for deterrence is the ability to pose such a threat that the thought of it will, in the mind of the adversary, outweigh any possible gains he might hope to acquire from aggressive action.

Secondly, though deterrence entails the risk of major casualties, human beings sometimes judge that the loss of many lives has been justified. In the war against Hitler, for example, some 50 million people died. It is true that the allies, in resisting, were not responsible for all these deaths. Most of them were attributable to Hitler and the Axis powers. But there is no escaping the fact that resistance, in a war that many of us would still regard as just, resulting in the loss of many lives. The Soviet Union, for example, lost nearly 20 million people in the defence of their country.[1] In Japan, if it had come to an invasion, there were 34,500,000 people trained to fight to the bitter end.[2] Anthony Kenny has written.

> There is something grotesque in the idea that because the allies were justified in going to war against Hitler, any war against a totalitarian enemy is justified if it causes fewer deaths than were lost in Hitler's war.[3]

Kenny is right to sound a note of caution about this type of argument, but two points need to be made. First, it is not, as was shown in the previous chapter, simply a question of deaths. In other words, what has to be weighed in the balance against the deaths that resulted from resisting Hitler is not just the deaths that Hitler, unimpeded, would have brought about (and the destriction of 7 million Jews was only a start) but a Nazi society poisoning human minds, including those of young children, with wicked values. Secondly, the argument is not 'because 50 million lost their lives fighting Hitler, we are justified in resisting other totalitarian regimes provided less than that number are killed'. That is a distortion. The point is to challenge or confirm the assumption that the use of nuclear weapons would automatically and inevitably be disproportionate. The fact is that people have and do think it morally worthwhile to suffer (and cause others to suffer) a great deal of destruction for the protection of societies which they believe express and preserve fundamental values like freedom. At what point the use of nuclear, or any other weapons, would become disproportionate is open to argument. But the second World War is a reminder that the use of nuclear weapons should not necessarily be judged out of all proportion to every possible end.

Chapters Seven and Eight showed that the principle of non-combatant immunity was central to the 'just war' tradition and argued for its validity in a nuclear age. Chapter Nine affirmed the principle of proportion as an essential tool of moral analysis. But is it in fact possible, with nuclear weapons, to have a targeting policy which, whilst it is effective for deterrence purposes, does not violate one or other of these principles?

First, deterrence does not depend on having more weapons than the other side or on the ability 'to prevail' in a nuclear war. It depends, quite simply, on ensuring that, whatever the circumstances, a potential enemy has more to lose than to gain by going to war. It depends on ensuring that an adversary contemplating war is always faced with an unacceptable risk.

Secondly, whatever targeting policy may have been in the past (due in part to cruder, less discriminating weapons) the point is that now and in the future it must be both discriminate and proportionate. Does present policy conform to these criteria and, if not, is it possible to evolve one that does, one which is still a credible deterrent?

Thirdly, although the principle of non-combatant immunity is, as we have argued, both valid and important, it is the principle of proportion and its implications that have to be examined most carefully. For many major cities could certainly be classified as military targets. They might contain a political base, a military command or an industrial complex capable of serving the military. The presence of such features would make such a city a legitimate target, in the sense that an attack on it would not constitute a direct attack on non-combatants. But, to put it in British terms, there may be very few cities, and those small, like Wells or Norwich or Carlisle which do not contain such features. In other words the principle of non-combatant immunity, by itself, may not act as much of a restraint. It could always be argued, by those who wished to, that an attack on Moscow or London or Birmingham was, despite massive civilian casualties, an attack on a military target. Therefore, without denying the validity of the principle of non-combatant immunity, it is the principle of proportion that comes to the fore, and with it the moral necessity of keeping loss of human life (even when the deaths are an unintended result of a direct attack on a military target) down to a minimum. For wars are fought to protect the harmless. The harmless of other countries (even those with whom we are at war) have as much moral claim on us as the harmless of our country, for whose protection we may have gone to war in the first place. A prime moral obligation in the nuclear age is therefore to evolve a targeting policy that minimizes loss of life rather than simply avoids attacking non-combatants *qua* non-combatants.

The strategy of the independent British deterrent, as stated in the 1981 *Open Government Document on Trident* (OGD 80/23) is that it should be:

> capable of posing a convincing threat — of inflicting on key aspects of Soviet state power, damage which any Soviet leadership would regard as out of all proportion to any likely gain from aggression against us.

'Key aspects of Soviet state power' is a phrase that could include everything from Moscow to a hydro-electric plant in Siberia. Nevertheless, although earlier British targeting policy seems to have been based on the need to penetrate the Galosh ABM screen around Moscow,[4] the capacity to do this need not be taken as a sign that we would do this if, tragically, deterrence failed. Michael Quinlan, then Deputy Under-Secretary of State in the Ministry of Defence, and at the heart of British nuclear planning, told a select committee of the

House of Commons in an examination of the Trident purchase in 1980:

> There is a concept which Chevaline makes clear, that Governments did not want to have a situation where the adversary could have a sanctuary for his capital and a large area around it.[5]

The wording of this 'Moscow criterion' is significant. It indicates the need for a capacity to hit Moscow without in any way implying that Moscow is or would be a target. Michael Quinlan, a Catholic much concerned with the morality of deterrence, has written, 'our planning need not and must not be genocidal; effective deterrence does not inescapably imply pure counter-population targeting'.[6]

Although the subject of targeting is highly secret there is some evidence that Britain has had a policy based on something other than simply destroying cities. In order to arrive at what this might be, it is worth asking two questions. One, what kind of threat would deter a country like Britain from aggressive action? And, two, what threat would dissuade a totalitarian country like the Soviet Union? It is possible, first to envisage an attack on a country like ours which, whilst not essentially counter-population, would cause such devastation to our economic life, our transport and communications, that the thought of it would deter us from aggression. Then, secondly, although a totalitarian state like the Soviet Union might be able to absorb much more destruction without being economically crippled, there are two other factors present. The Soviet Union is a vast country, comprising about a fifth of the earth's surface and composed of a hundred or so distinct nationalities and languages. It is amazing how the Soviet Union achieves any kind of social cohesion. When this is taken together with the fact that the majority of the population are probably secretly but sullenly hostile to the regime, and that some of the minority groups have potential for great disruption, e.g. the Islamic communities, it is possible to see how a threat to their capacity for internal control would be a major threat. This would point to a targeting policy which aimed not only at economic disruption but at centres of control and communication within the USSR, together with attacks on military establishments that rendered useless any capacity for external conquest and occupation. Such a plan would be highly threatening to a Marxist–Leninist regime that was, at the best of times, uncertain about its ability to rule except by force.

There is no doubt, however, that even such a targeting policy, one that sought to avoid attacks on heavily populated areas, would cause massive casualties. Could this possibly be proportionate? At this point judgement will inevitably vary. All, no doubt, would agree that 100 million dead would be unacceptable. Many would say that 1 million dead, however, would be a lesser evil than the alternative. But what about 20 million? It is, however, important to note that these are targeting plans, not orders to fire, and these exist precisely in order to maximize the chance that they will never have to be used in reality.

Nevertheless, it is argued, though there might conceivably be some theoretical targets for nuclear weapons that would not be disproportionate, any actual use would rapidly escalate into a war that *would* be disproportionate. For example, the use of tactical nuclear weapons on a tank formation might in theory be proportionate, but, once the nuclear firebreak had been crossed, further exchanges would quickly take place causing destruction that no conceivable good could justify.

The thought that if nuclear weapons were ever used there would be a rapid escalation to an all–out nuclear exchange played a crucial role in both *The Church and the Bomb* and *The Challenge of Peace*. Whatever initial sympathy there might have been for the idea that there could be a just use of nuclear weapons was rapidly dispelled by the prospect of escalation. It was judged, in both reports, that escalation to uses of nuclear weapons that would be grossly disproportionate was vitually inevitable. But is escalation as inevitable as the authors of these reports suggest? And even if there is a genuine risk of escalation, as of course there is, should this be allowed to be the overriding factor. In many quarters the thinking of these reports on escalation has been accepted somewhat uncritically.

First, it must be asserted that escalation is not an automatic process nor must it be allowed to become such. Whatever the anger and confusion of war, there are still moral decision to be made by human beings.

Secondly, if, tragically, deterrence failed and war broke out so that nuclear weapons were used, the pressure on both sides to halt the war and resolve their differences as quickly as possible would be enormous. A real possibility is that the terrible destruction brought about by even one such weapon would create a sense of shock and horror and a corresponding determination to stop further explosions. No political leadership could contemplate with equanimity the destruction of its own country. There would be the strongest possible motive for bringing active hostilities to a juddering halt.

Thirdly, whatever thoughts an aggressor might have had in initiating hostilities, the use of nuclear weapons against him would be bound to bring about a rapid reappraisal of his situation. Aggression would have commenced on the assumption that likely gains would outweigh the possible risks; that he could obtain what he wanted at an acceptable cost. If nuclear weapons were used by the defender it would force the aggressor to conclude that he had miscalculated the balance of advantage; that he had underestimated the resolve of the other side and that, if the war·continued, it could only lead to suicide. This conclusion is further reinforced by considering the only scenario in which NATO would contemplate using nuclear weapons, that is, if its homelands were about to be overrun. Then the NATO countries would have everything to fight for, for their very existence was at stake. For an aggressor, however, no such vital interest would be at stake. It is hardly likely he would go further and risk his heartland for something which was less than vital. All the pressure would be on coming to some kind of accommodation before another shot was fired.

Against this it has been suggested that the Soviet Union has no intention of using nuclear weapons in any limited way. If the West once used its weapons, of however low a yield, this would unleash the full might of the Soviet nuclear armoury. It is quite true that this is the stated Soviet position. But they have a particular reason for wanting to maintain that position in public, namely to deter first use of nuclear weapons by NATO. They have no interest in encouraging the idea that a limited and controlled use of nuclear weapons is possible, precisely the opposite. In fact, however, the general considerations mentioned in previous paragraphs apply no less to the Soviet leadership than to any other, indeed perhaps more, for since the second World War that leadership has shown itself to be notably cautious, probing western reactions but not putting pressure on to the point of war. Furthermore, whatever Soviet declaratory policy may be, for the reason already mentioned, they do in fact have a capability for controlled and disciplined use of nuclear weapons. It is difficult to conceive of any circumstances in which they would want to overthrow all restraints.

The considerations so far apply to the likelihood of controlled escalation. There is, however, also the spectre of uncontrolled escalation. In the fog and bitterness of war, perhaps the political leadership would lose control and the nuclear battle take on a momentum of its own under local commanders. Yet, despite the possibility of this, there are strong pressures against such an outcome. For it could hardly be in the interest of any political leadership to lose control of their own nuclear forces. Combined with this, the procedures for nuclear release are so complex and secure that, even in the event of a loss of communication, local commanders are not at liberty to order a nuclear strike. Then, in relation to the forces of the other side, there is a strong interest in a targeting policy that tries to ensure that the other side does *not* totally lose control of its nuclear forces. For in the tragic event of deterrence failing the compelling priority would be to bring hostilities to a stop as soon as possible. For this to be done it would be necessary to have a political leadership with which to deal and, moreover, one that was still in control of its own nuclear forces. Thus whilst it would be possible to have an effective targeting policy based upon disrupting the Soviet Union's control over its heartland and its capacity for aggression i.e. directed mainly to its conventional forces, there is a strong disincentive to destroying the enemy's control over its nuclear forces.

In addition to these practical considerations which show

that escalation, far from being inevitable, is one possible outcome amongst others, there is a moral dimension to the argument. Could it ever be right to allow the fear of escalation to paralyse all resistance to perceived aggression? If, when someone was attacked, they did not resist for fear that their resistance would result in the attacker grabbing a weapon, this might be prudent under those particular circumstances. But if this fear was made a principle, it would result in no resistance ever being offered, for resistance always carries the risk that the attacker will make his attack that much more ferocious. This scruple would leave the world at the mercy of those prepared to use force to gain what they wanted. Or, if resistance was offered but only up to a certain point, this would leave the world at the mercy of the most ruthless and unscrupulous powers. What is in question of course is resistance by morally acceptable means. The pacifist believes that only verbal persuasion or indirect coercion are morally tolerable. The nuclear pacifist believes that only conventional forces may be used. If those judgements are made, they must be respected. But the effect is the same in both cases: the world is at the mercy of the power that has retained nuclear weapons and the will to use them if need be. This too is a factor of the utmost *moral* importance which has to be weighed against the risk of having to use nuclear weapons.

In recent years the governments of the world have on the whole united to combat hijacking of aircraft by terrorists. It has been generally agreed that terrorists must not be allowed to get away with blackmail, even though this often means putting the lives of innocent passengers at risk. The local forces are often faced with a terrible dilemma, where the lives of many passengers do seem to be in grave danger. But the alternative is worse, allowing terrorists to think that if only they raise the stakes high enough their demands will be met. The same principle used to resist terrorists holds in relations between states. It could never be moral to encourage a situation in which a government was allowed to think that if only it made the risk to innocent life grave enough, it could obtain what it wanted.

There is always a risk of escalation, and this is true at every level of resistance. Even if all nuclear use had been disavowed but nuclear weapons were still possessed for deterrence purposes, the risk of escalation from the use of conventional to nuclear weapons would still be present. A knowledge of this risk is not a bad thing. It helps to underpin deterrence. Any aggressor knows that he cannot calculate precisely that the gains would outweigh the risks. He might attack with conventional forces believing he would be met only with conventional resistance which he could defeat. But he would be taking the risk that, if defeated, the other side would use nuclear weapons against him, and this could lead to all-out use. The risk ensures that no potential adversary is ever in a position to say that the probable gains will outweigh possible risks. Moreover, as has been argued, escalation is not automatic, it is not the only possibility if deterrence fails: and, even though there is a grave risk, it would be totally wrong, on moral grounds, to allow this risk to paralyse all resistance.

In applying the principle of proportion we have to assess risks, of which the risk of escalation, if a war broke out, is one. But this is not the only risk or the only factor to be considered in making up one's mind about the morality of nuclear deterrence. The main considerations are:
(1) the stability or instability of deterrence,
(2) the risk of escalation if deterrence failed,
(3) the nature of the hostile regime by which one might be subjugated,
(4) the intentions of that regime on the international scene,
(5) the extent of likely devastation if a war took place.
Taking the fifth point first, there need be no disagreement about this. Many scientific studies have been made, the results of which appear in most books on this subject. The results of even a partial exchange of nuclear weapons would be quite terrible. There is no dispute about what these weapons can do. The question is how to stop them ever being used. The fourth point is more controversial. There are those who believe that the Soviet Union intends to invade western Europe. That is not my view. Marxist-Leninism is still a crusading ideology bent on world domination, but the Soviet Union does not see itself imposing this ideology on Europe by force. On the other hand, for reasons suggested in Chapter

Three, benign intentions are not enough. Moreover, if coercion became an easy option, then sooner or later a power (especially one with weak internal mechanisms of self-restraint, like the Soviet Union) might come to feel exploitative inclinations which, perhaps genuinely, are not currently in its mind. It is the nature of large states to expand their power and influence if they can. The third point is, again, more controversial. But it is not necessary to be 'soft' on the Soviet Union in order to oppose deterrence. There are those who are well aware of the nature of a Marxist-Leninist regime and who still oppose deterrence on moral grounds.[7] Another point about which one needs to be careful is not to equate the Soviet Union now with what it was under Stalin. On the other hand, it would be foolish to forget that there is very little in the way of checks and balances in the Soviet system to prevent a Stalinist regime from achieving power again.

On the second point, it has already been argued that the risk of escalation, though very grave, is not a foregone conclusion. There is no question of underestimating the risk. It is a very serious one. As Sydney Bailey and others emphasize, the pressure of time, previous targeting policy and the sorry example of other wars make a sombre picture. But, for reasons already adduced, it is not certain. There are other possibilities, and for moral reasons it cannot be allowed to be the overriding factor. It is an extremely grave factor that has to be taken into account with other factors and other risks. This leaves the first, and perhaps most fundamental judgement of all. How stable is deterrence? For if deterrence is fundamentally stable, other risks can be taken. Paul Oestreicher, a firm opponent of deterrence on moral grounds, has said in public that if he believed deterrence was 100 per cent safe he would support it despite all his moral objections on other grounds. Nothing is 100 per cent safe; nevertheless deterrence is, I believe, fundamentally robust. And this is affirmed even by some of those who are strongly against it on moral grounds, such as Sydney Bailey. The reason for believing that deterrence is essentially stable, in other words that there is only a remote chance of a major war between the superpowers, despite all the rhetoric, has little to do with trust in human goodness. It is the fact that for the first time in human history it could not be in the interest of one of the superpowers to go to war with the other. Nations go to war because they judge they have something to gain by doing so. What power could gain by going to war against another power that possessed nuclear weapons? Some writers argue that, whereas deterrence was once stable, now it is so no longer because of new more accurate missiles capable of 'taking out' enemy missiles and because of the multiplication of 'fight the war' strategies.[8] But these fears ignore one fundamental fact: the existence of submarine based missiles. Submarines containing nuclear missiles are virtually untrackable and are likely to remain so for the forseeable future. This means that even if all the land based missiles of one power were destroyed on site, that power would still have an assured second strike capacity. It is just conceivable that at some point in the future technology will advance to the state when submarines in the depths of the ocean can be accurately located and destroyed and that this can be achieved simultaneously for all submarines in the ocean at any one time. This is remarkably demanding and correspondingly remote, but if it became possible the situation would change and deterrence might cease to be the stable factor that it is now. But for the present and foreseeable future there is an assured second strike capacity and deterrence is inherently stable. If this was not the case it could not be supported.

In considering nuclear deterrence we have to consider the likelihood of certain events, such as deterrence failing, or escalation taking place; and also the goods and evils that have to be weighed, the values preserved in our society or the values denied in a Marxist-Leninist society. Some have sought to resolve these equations by quasi-mathematical means. Others have tried to short-cut such considerations altogether. For example, Anthony Kenny believes they can be resolved by a Pascal type of wager:

> Pascal maintained that we ought to believe in God because the penalties for not believing in him if he existed amounted to infinite loss, while the penalty for believing in him if he did not exist was merely a degree of modest but unnecessary self-discipline. Similarly, the

worst case outcome of deterrence, namely nuclear devastation, is so much more catastrophic than the worst case outcome of disarmament, Russian domination, that the course which leads to it should be avoided no matter what the relative probabilities of the two outcomes of the different strategies.[9]

This is a weak argument. First, it can be questioned whether even the horror of a major nuclear exchange is the worst evil we can think of. In George Orwell's *1984*, Winston Smith and his girl-friend believe they can defeat the society about them. Although they know they will be caught and killed, they think they can win if only they die hating the system. The pathos of the novel is that, as a result of the ruthless brainwashing, they die loving big brother. We would have to say that such a society, if it ever came into being, would be the worst evil we could imagine, because the very possibility of being human would no longer exist. This is not to suggest that any society now conforms to that depicted in *1984*. It does not, though the potential for becoming such a society is always present when a Marxist-Leninist ideology is dominant. The point is, however, that it is not axiomatic that even a nuclear war is the worst evil we can imagine. How we should act will depend on risks and probabilities. If we were faced with the takeover of our society in a way which would turn it into one similar to that in *1984*, and this was, on all human predictions, certain, but we had a good chance of averting this through maintaining a system of deterrence, we should of course choose the latter. In fact, of course, the situation is much more complex than that. The Soviet Union is not the society of *1984* nor are we about to be taken over by it. There is, further, some risk, however slight, of deterrence failing. The point is, however, to challenge the widely held assumption that taking the risk of a nuclear exchange is the worst possible evil.

Secondly, if I had fought in World War 2, I would have feared capture by the Japanese. I would have feared being totally humiliated and betraying my friends. This is my worst conceivable fear, far outweighing all others. But does this mean that I should have refused to fight because this would

involve a risk that I would be sent to the Far East? The fact is
that there is no way of short cutting the assessment of risks
and weighing up of values. There is no mathematical way of
doing this either. It is a matter of human political judgement.
Grotius has a detailed discussion of what to do if good and
evil consequences are equally mixed, or one is more likely to
come about than the other and so on, but in the end he comes
back to a homely analogy. Doctors cure slight diseases by
slight means 'but in more grave diseases are compelled to
apply dangerous and doubtful remedies'.[10] It is a reminder
that the decisions we make about likelihood and values are
not confined to war.

From the time of Suarez,[11] it has been generally accepted
that for a war to be just there must be a reasonable chance of
victory. This is, as was suggested earlier, a logical extension
of the principle of proportion. It was also urged that, in our
time, it made sense to apply the principle to defensive as well
as offensive war. Some have argued that because there are no
winners in an all-out nuclear exchange the threat to use
nuclear weapons fails this criteria of the 'just war' tradition as
well as others. It is important, however, not to treat the 'just
war' criteria woodenly. For example, an eminent Catholic
jurist argued, at the time that the Portuguese held a number of
colonies in Africa, that the liberation movements failed 'just
war' criteria because they had no chance of success.[12] Almost
as the book was published and almost overnight, the
Portuguese empire collapsed. The author had failed to grasp
the nature of guerrilla war, that it is primarily a political
struggle. It is not necessary to win great military victories. All
that is necesary is to stay in business and be enough of a
nuisance until the political victory is won. Similarly, in
applying the criterion of 'reasonable chance of success' to
nuclear weapons, we have to understand what it is that we are
primarily talking about. It is indeed true that there would be
no victors in an all-out nuclear exchange, and this is one of the
factors that contribute to deterrence. If deterrence failed, the
urgent priority on both sides would be to bring the war to a
halt as rapidly as possible. But the criteria of success is
applicable primarily to the dissuasive effect of the deployment
of nuclear weapons. If their deployment ensures that an

aggressor desists from attacking, then the deploying power has in a key sense succeeded. For deterrence has replaced war as the fundamental fact about the relationship between two super powers. This point can hardly be overstated and in its light almost everything has to be rethought. If the deployment of nuclear weapons continues to dissuade, that is, if deterrence is fundamentally stable, then the criterion of success is more than adequately met. In the judgement of many experts deterrence is exceedingly robust, for reasons indicated in the next chapter. It is a judgement I share.

Notes

1. Geoffrey Hosking, *A History of the Soviet Union,* Fontana, 1985, Chapter 10.
2. Leonard Cheshire, *The Light of Many Suns,* Methuen 1985, p.30.
3. Anthony Kenny, *The Logic of Deterrence,* Firethorn Press, 1985, p.42.
4. Lawrence Freedman, 'British Nuclear Targeting', in *Defence Analysis,* Volume 1, No.2, pp.81–99.
5. House of Commons Defence Committee, *Strategic Nuclear Weapons Policing,* p.107.
6. Michael Quinlan, 'The Meaning of Deterrence' in *The Cross and the Bomb,* ed. F. Bridger, Mowbray, 1983, p.152.
7. e.g. Anthony Kenny.
8. Frank Barnaby in *Dropping the Bomb,* ed. J. Gladwin, Hodder & Stoughton, 1985, Chapter 2.
9. *The Logic of Deterrence,* p.63.
10. *De iure belli ac pacis,* 2, 24, 5, 4.
11. Suarez argues with Cajetan about what degree of likelihood of victory is necessary; but the texts that he refers to in Catejan deal with another subject.
12. John Epstein, *Does God say kill?,* Stacey, 1972.

CHAPTER ELEVEN

Deterrence and its nuclear component

The word deterrence has become virtually synonymous with the concept of nuclear deterrence. This is highly misleading, for whatever differences of opinion there may be about *nuclear* deterrence, deterrence in one form or another is fundamental to human life. Deterrence rests on two assumptions which few would deny. First, in the world as we have it there are individuals, groups and nations who will try to obtain what they want at the expense of others. Secondly, these individuals, groups and nations pursue what they see to be in their interest and, on the whole, will not harm other people if the risk of hurt to themselves outweighs possible advantages. Far more is involved in deterrence than the capacity to inflict pain. A burglar alarm on a house deters because it suggests to potential intruders that they are likely to get caught. Similarly an unarmed policemen walking down a street deters potential muggers. So also a father walking back with his daughter across a common deters. As has often been observed, justly, the likelihood of being caught is a far greater deterrent to criminals than any talk of extended prison sentences or hanging. Two elements that are fundamental to any form of deterrence may therefore be singled out. Neither have anything to do with nuclear weapons as such.

First and most fundamental of all is the will to resist and the communication of this willingness to potential aggressors. This was discussed in Chapter Four, where the judgement of General Wolf Von Baudisin about the French lack of will to resist the German invasion was mentioned. This will must not only be present, however, it must also be signalled to others. It was the failure to do this that brought about the classic failure of deterrence in our time, the Argentine invasion of the Falkland Islands. We did in fact have the will to resist, as was subsequently shown at some cost. What we

134

failed to do, however, was to convey clearly to the Argentinians at the right time that we were so determined. In fact, we conveyed quite the opposite impression. We let the Argentinians think that we were not interested in defending the islands and that if they invaded they could get away with it at little cost to themselves. Parents blame children for leaving bicycles around unpadlocked in a public place where they are likely to be stolen. We left an island unpadlocked in a hostile sea.

The Falklands war was the tragic consequence of failure by successive British political parties. One good, however, did come out of it. It strengthened deterrence everywhere. It indicated to the world as a whole that we had the will and resolve to resist armed aggression from wherever it might come. It is on this resolve, more than on anything else, that deterrence is based.

The first necessity for an effective deterrence is the will to resist. The second is the means to do so. This carries with it the further corollaries, that the means could actually be used, and any potential enemy would or might well believe they would be used. These corollaries are crucial in the nuclear age because of doubts raised on precisely these grounds. Could NATO ever risk using nuclear weapons, and does the USSR believe they would (and vice versa)? In order to meet these doubts, two developments have taken place. First, over the years, NATO has evolved a policy of flexible response. Obviously, the details of this are complex, but the essential idea is that NATO should be able to meet any threat offered with the appropriate response and should not immediately be forced into the position of using strategic nuclear weapons. The policy of flexible response has come in for a great deal of ill-informed criticism. But it is an entirely logical attempt to meet two vital aims; first, to make deterrence credible, in other words, to ensure that we could actually use some of the weapons at our disposal, and, secondly, to make the risk of going to war against NATO outweigh any conceivable advantage. These twin aims are achieved by having an **adequate** conventional capability which could offer effective resistance, and by having a whole range of options between the use of conventional force and an all-out nuclear exchange, so that any potential aggressor was bound to fear that he might set in motion a train of escalation which would bring disaster upon him. The existence of an effective conventional force underpins the credibility of deterrence, whilst a policy of flexible response ensures that the defence system as a whole deters under all circumstances.

The second development that has begun to take place in order to meet the doubts raised about NATO's capacity to deter, is the strengthening of its conventional forces, especially through emerging technology (ET). Ever since NATO went over to nuclear weapons, which they did in part on grounds of cost, there have been critics of this excessive reliance on nuclear weapons. People like Professor Michael Howard have continually argued for a strengthening of conventional forces, and in principle NATO has agreed to it. The difficulty has been cost, coupled with the sheer size of the Warsaw Pact conventional forces. Now, for the first time, it looks as though it might be possible, through ET, to have a conventional force that was adequate without vastly increasing manpower and which, whilst expensive, could over a period of years be afforded. The new technology makes it possible for targets to be precisely located and, then, for weapons to be delivered to those targets with pin-point accuracy. For example, a tank formation could be spotted and then cluster bombs delivered so that an explosive warhead would home in on each individual tank. Or an aircraft runway could be located and precision-guided weapons used so that bombs went off at regular intervals all along the tarmac, thereby rendering it unusable.[1]

The deployment of this emerging technology is not without its controversial side. In the minds of some people it is associated with so-called air-land battle plans that involve deep strikes into Soviet held territory. These attacks on second and third echelon forces (follow on forces attack: FOFA) would, it is argued, immobilize any Soviet attack. For this and other reasons the Soviet Union has been hostile to the development of these weapons by the West. Further discussion of these weapons and possible tactics associated with their use would go too far outside the scope of this study. But the strengthening of conventional forces is to be welcomed for a number of reasons. First, it strengthens deterrence. The purpose of having a more effective conventional force is not to make conventional wars more likely but to make deterrence more credible. Lawrence Freedman has written:

> the criticism of a conventional strategy, that it somehow makes war more manageable and predictable, and so a more tolerable option for an aggressor, is misplaced. In practice, a strengthening of conventional forces strengthens pure deterrence, by ensuring that an aggressor cannot predict with confidence the result of a clash of forces in the centre of Europe.[2]

The second advantage of strengthening conventional forces is that it makes it possible to become less reliant on nuclear weapons, thereby raising the nuclear threshold. This would come about as a result of the two main consequences of deploying ET. First, tasks for which until now it has been necessary to employ a nuclear device, would be performed by conventional weapons. A relatively small conventional explosive precisely on the target would replace a much larger nuclear blast obliterating a whole area. So the range of targets for which it might be necessary to employ nuclear weapons is cut down. Secondly, because targets can be accurately located and weapons can be precisely directed at them, such nuclear weapons as are still deemed necessary on the battlefield can be placed much further back, thereby rendering them that much less vulnerable and prone to use-or-lose pressures. Because of these two effects of using ET, NATO has been able to plan to reduce its tactical nuclear weapons by 35 per cent. Whether or not NATO ever achieves a position in which it would never have to contemplate using nuclear weapons first, it is obviously highly desirable that it becomes less dependent on such weapons or their early use. Even if the Soviet Union develops ET, as in the course of time is likely, it is argued that this type of weapon favours the defender. For one predicted effect of their deployment is to inhibit mobility on both sides and it is generally held that aggressors need mobility more than defenders.

It is important on both practical and moral grounds that

NATO becomes less dependent on nuclear weapons; that they achieve a position where they no longer have to contemplate using nuclear weapons early in a war. This position, an actual policy of no-early-use with concomitant changes in deployment and training, is not to be used with a declaratory policy of no-first-use, for which many Churches have called. A declaratory policy, as the phrase suggests, is one in which we declare beforehand that under no circumstances would we use nuclear weapons first. The purpose of making such a declaration would be to elicit more trust from the other side. But it is a misconceived idea. By implication it conceives modern warfare as a kind of game, which can be played up to but not beyond certain limits, whereas in fact it is just the opposite. Furthermore, it could conceivably tempt an aggressor to think that he could risk an attack and obtain what he wanted at an acceptable risk. If a statement of no-first-use was made, one could only hope that the other side would *not* believe it. A declaratory policy of no-first-use also misconceives the nature of conflict in a nuclear age. It is not simply nuclear use that has to be avoided but war itself. It is war, particularly a conventional war in central Europe, that has to be deterred. War of any kind, including a conventional attack that escalated into a nuclear exchange, is more likely to be deterred by *not* having a declaratory policy of no-first use.[3] But this is not to be confused, as has been said, with an actual policy of no-early use which is highly desirable on both moral and practical grounds. The imperative is to so strengthen our conventional capability that we are less dependent on nuclear weapons and their early use in a war.

A number of rather different justifications for a policy of nuclear deterrence have been evolved, not all of them convincing. Some argue, for example, that, whilst it would be immoral ever actually to use such weapons, their retention for deterrence purposes is the least evil course of action at present open to us. There are two strands of truth in this position. The first is that all deterrence depends on working on the minds of potential adversaries, and there is no exact relation between what they believe you might do and what you are committed in advance to do. Secondly if, tragically, deterrence did fail and a war broke out, this would be a different situation from that which prevailed before. On both prudential and moral grounds, we might be required to act in a different manner from the one which had been implied before and on the basis of which the enemy had calculated we would behave. Nevertheless, to leave a chasm between possession and use is highly unsatisfactory, also on both practical and moral grounds. From a practical point of view it is difficult to see how deterrence could continue to work. Deterrence depends on convincing a potential adversary that, under certain circumstances, nuclear weapons might be used against him. If our policy were truly one of pure bluff, this would in the end betray itself. From a moral point of view, it is difficult to see how a country could justify training men and women to use nuclear weapons and deploying them to do so, if what they are being asked to contemplate doing is immoral. Common sense and common morality combine to suggest that a deterrence policy must be based on the possibility that under certain circumstances a nuclear weapon could actually be used.

Debate has taken place in recent years about whether, even if all use of nuclear weapons was judged to be immoral, retaining the option of using them with the intention of avoiding ever having to use them, is also immoral. These discussions have raised the question of what is intended in nuclear deterrence, as well as complex philosophical problems about the nature of intention. It was suggested in the discussion on double effect in Chapter Eight that what we intend is more than the most immediate consequences of an action. If you shoot to kill someone, it is hardly an excuse to say you only intended to pull the trigger. On the other hand, the notion of intention loses all meaning if you try to include very long term consequences of an action. In order to judge the intention of an action, we have to take some of its immediate consequences into account such as the pulling of the trigger, the trajectory of the bullet, the point of impact and so on: but not every consequence. The hiring of the undertakers, the mourning of the widow and the claims on the insurance company are not usually relevant. In the light of this what is the intention of a system of deterrence?

The primary intention of deterrence is to dissuade a

potential adversary from initiating armed hostilities. This primary intention is, however, dependent on a secondary intention, to convince an adversary that there are circumstances in which nuclear weapons might be used against them. For this, it is not necessary to retain an actual intention to use the weapons. All that is required is that we retain the option of possible use in such a way that a potential adversary believes nuclear weapons could be used against him if he committed an aggressive act. This secondary intention is, however, dependent on a judgement that not every possible use of nuclear weapons would violate the principles of discrimination and proportion.[4] It has been argued in earlier chapters that this is indeed the case. Not every conceivable use of nuclear weapons would violate the principle of discrimination and proportion. Nor, as was argued, can the prospect of escalation be allowed to become the overriding consideration.

A strategy of nuclear deterrence is in essence a simple idea but it has a number of facets that are not always taken into account. It depends on having both the resolution to resist and the appropriate means with which to do so. From this springs the need for:

i) an adequate conventional capability. Here ET has been a help.

ii) a flexible enough policy so that when faced with an attack at less than strategic level we would never be pushed into the position of having to choose between using strategic weapons or submitting to the adversary. This is in fact a practical application of the principle of proportion. If an enemy launched a conventional attack there must be a conventional capability strong enough to deny it the prospect of rapid or assured success. If they used low yield nuclear weapons on military targets, the adversary must have the capability to do the same.

Nevertheless, nuclear deterrence does *not* depend on a positive decision made in advance, to use nuclear weapons. It is constituted by the following factors. First, the very possession of nuclear weapons is a deterrent. Even if we made a public statement to the effect that we would never use them (which it would not be prudent or moral to make) a potential enemy would never be absolutely sure. Even if, as a matter of morality, we made a firm but secret policy decision to avoid major attacks on or near heavily populated areas and an adversary discovered this, he could never be sure we meant what we intended.

Secondly, there is the deterrent effect of targeting plans that envisage a discriminate and proportionate use of nuclear weapons. As was argued earlier it is possible to have an effective deterrence which does not depend on essentially counter-population targeting policy. It is possible to envisage uses of nuclear weapons which, whilst well able to deter a potential aggressor, would not necessarily be either indiscriminate or disproportionate. At the very least, such discriminate and proportionate uses could not be ruled out *a priori*, which is all that is necessary for a deterrent strategy that is moral. Such deterrent strategy carries with it a corresponding moral obligation to ensure not only that it *could* be carried out within the bounds of discrimination and proportionality but that it *would* be. British and NATO targeting policy is of course a subject that is shrouded in secrecy. Nevertheless, there is a duty to raise the question and to press the obligation to achieve a policy that is moral. A targeting policy that was essentially counter-city or which envisaged weapons of high yield being exploded on military targets in densely populated areas would run counter to the whole thrust of 'just war' thinking. As has been argued, it is possible to have an effective deterrent strategy that does not depend on such targets. It is a moral imperative to ensure that it does not so depend.

Thirdly, there is the wholesome fear of escalation. Whilst escalation, if deterrence tragically failed, is certainly not wanted, so long as deterrence holds the possibility of escalation has good consequences. The thought of it increases caution and a sense of prudence in anyone tempted to start a war.

Nuclear weapons have only one, limited but crucial function, and that is to deter other powers that possess nuclear weapons. Nuclear weapons are not weapons like other weapons. They are not there for fighting or winning wars. Nuclear war in the traditional sense cannot be won. This is the Copernican revolution that has taken place in our time. The only purpose of possessing such weapons is to prevent a war being fought. What is needed is a minimum deterrence. As has been argued, deterrence depends on the ability to convince a potential adversary that the risks of aggression outweigh any possible benefits. An effective conventional capacity, combined with some nuclear weapons and a policy of flexible response, ensures that this can be done whatever form the hostile action might take. There is no point in overkill. Indeed the piling up of nuclear weapons is likely to undermine public confidence in the deterrence system. If deterrence is stable, why this need for more and more? On moral grounds, the general principle that is applicable to the fighting of a war is applicable also to the deployment of force to ensure that wars do not have to be fought. What is strictly necessary may be done but *only* that which is strictly necessary may be done. The retention of a nuclear component is necessary for deterrence purposes: but only that which is necessary for deterrence may be deployed.

Despite all that has been said, a certain unease must remain with anyone of a sensitive conscience about the retention of even some of these weapons. When we contemplate what they *could* do, our instinctive reaction is to have nothing whatever to do with them, to divest ourselves of them as quickly as possible. But what would that mean? It would leave nuclear weapons in the possession of one side alone. Would that be conducive to justice and peace? There are those who say that such an act of renunciation would kindle an answering act of trust in the other camp. That is not my judgement. As was discussed earlier, states do not act like individuals. States seek to maximize their own power, where they can do so without undue risk. Particularly this is the case with the USSR, which retains its mission to bring communism to the world. But it would also be true of the United States. The United States, no less than other powers in human history, seeks to maximize its influence and power overseas. Although at the moment this power is exercised to block communist expansion, even without that ideology to oppose, the United States would be interested in an expansion of its markets, its prestige and its friends. The most benign power in the world is still experienced by lesser powers as powerful. It would be fair to acknowledge that the United States did have a monopoly of nuclear power for a decade or more after the Second World War and did not use it coercively. But no nation could be trusted indefinitely in that position.

The complete renunciation of nuclear weapons by one superpower so that all the nuclear weapons in the world were left in the hands of the other superpower, could be the first step towards a world tyranny. Given a world where differences of perception and interest are permanent and in which quarrels arising from these differences are always a possibility, what would there be to stop the one nuclear power in the world from eventually imposing its will on the world as a whole? Furthermore, if that power conceived its historic mission as bringing its ideology to the world as a whole, such a monopoly of absolute power could hardly be viewed with equanimity.

For this reason, and despite all the serious reservations about the morality of use, the most weighty Church bodies have affirmed deterrence to be morally acceptable under certain conditions. This was the judgement of the American Roman Catholic bishops. Their view, like that of conferences of Roman Catholic bishops elsewhere in the world, has understandably been guided by the now famous statement that the Pope made in June 1982 at the United Nations Second Special Session on Disarmament.

> In current conditions 'deterrence' based on balance, certainly not as an end in itself but as a stage on the way toward a progressive disarmament, may still be judged morally acceptable.

Yet, despite the influence of that statement, the motion agreed by the Church of England at its synod on 10 February 1983 is sounder, affirming as it does that maintaining adequate forces is not simply acceptable but a duty. The synod affirmed:

> it is the duty of HM Government and her allies to maintain adequate forces to guard against nuclear

blackmail and to deter potential nuclear and non-nuclear aggressors.

Notes

1. For a description of what is possible with ET see Hugh Beach, 'Military Implications of "No First Use"' in *Dropping the Bomb,* ed. John Gladwin, Hodder & Stoughton, 1985, pp.51-59. See also Hugh Beach's 'Disarmament and Security in Europe' in *Armed Peace,* ed. Josephine O'Conner Howe, Macmillan, 1984, pp.7-30.
2. Lawrence Freedman, 'The Conventional Option' in *What Hope in an Armed World?,* ed. Richard Harries, Pickering & Inglis, 1982, p.48.
3. See my article 'Nuclear Weapons: The General Synod Decision in the Light of Day', in *Crucible,* April-June 1983.
4. See a good discussion by David Fisher, *Morality and the Bomb,* Chapter Six.

CHAPTER TWELVE

War in space

In March 1983 President Reagan announced to the world that the United States was embarking on a research project which, for the first time, might offer a defence against nuclear weapons. This SDI (Strategic Defence Initiative) is of great significance and has changed the terms of the strategic debate. As can be seen from the diagram the plan is for a multi-layered defence system which would attack incoming missiles in each of the four missile phases with directed energy weapons (DEWs). The four phases are:

Phase 1: the boost phase, lasting some 3–5 minutes, in which the missile is carried above the atmosphere by multi-stage booster rocket engines which produce an intense and unique infra-red signature.

Phase 2: the post-boost phase, sometimes called the 'bussing' phase, lasting a further 7–10 minutes during which the payload separates itself from the engines. This payload typically dispenses re-entry vehicles carrying nuclear warheads, each released sequentially to follow the targeting path encoded into it and also a cloud of penetration aids (marked 'Penaids' on the diagram) designed to baffle the defence, decoys with a similar radar signature to that of the re-entry vehicles, balloons enclosing MIRVs (multiple independent re-entry vehicles) or decoys or nothing at all, radar-reflecting wires called chaff or infra-red-emitting aerosols.

Phase 3: the mid-course phase, during which the MIRVs and the penetration aids would follow virtually identical trajectories.

Phase 4: the terminal phases of re-entry into the atmosphere, during which the penetration aids would be slowed down or destroyed.

The technical problems of achieving such a defence are enormous. We have become so used to 'star wars' scenarios in films and books and adjusted to the idea that science can solve any problem that there is a tendency to underestimate the extent of the problem of erecting a defensive shield in space. There are a number of distinguished scientists who doubt whether it can in fact be done. One of the problems has to do with generating enough energy on a satellite battle station to achieve a laser or particle beam of enough strength and accuracy to destroy incoming missiles. Another problem is the sheer speed at which everything would have to work. Because of the difficulty of generating enough energy in space another idea which has been suggested is of a 'pop-up' satellite. A submarine near the Soviet Union would shoot up a satellite to the height at which an enemy missile started to bend round the earth and would shoot it down from there. But the crucial boost phase of a missile, when the missile can be clearly discerned in the atmosphere is short. The American MX missile, for example, takes only between 150 and 180 seconds. The pop-up interceptor from a submarine could reach the target sighting point in about 120 seconds. That does not leave much time — and with some adjustments it has been calculated it would be possible to reduce the time of the boost phase of an MX missile to as little as 60 seconds. This brings out a fundamental point. Even if the technical difficulties of a ballistic missile defence (BMD) in space could be solved, counter measures can be taken for far less cost. There are a whole range of counter measures that could be developed. One has been mentioned, shortening the crucial boost phase of the missile. Another idea is to make the boost erratic. For a laser beam to be effective it has to fasten on to the target and stay there. If the missile is not only moving but moving with different speeds at different times in an unpredictable way, the beams would be ineffective. Another scheme is for the hardening of the missile, so that the laser beam could not penetrate it. Other devices could be adopted at different stages of the missiles' flight path. As already mentioned, in the so called bussing phase, when the MIRVs have been released, there could be a whole series of penetration aids. There would be a whole swarm of objects, all of which, however light, would move along the missile trajectory, indistinguishable from the weapons themselves. Above all, an adversary could simply increase the number of

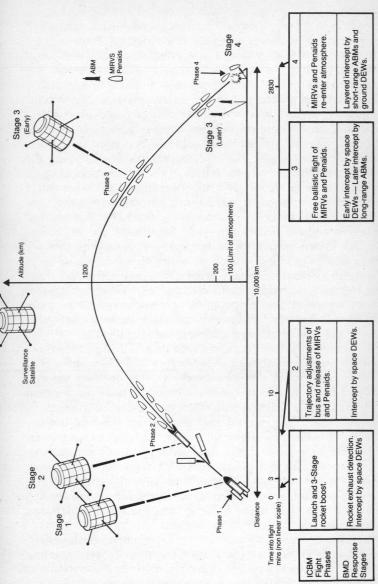

Figure 1 Schematic Representation of Multi-layered Ballistic Missile Defence System.

ICBM Flight Phases				
Time into flight mins (non linear scale)	0 3	10		2830
	Phase 1	Phase 2	Phase 3	Phase 4

BMD Response Stages				
	1	2	3	4
	Launch and 3-Stage rocket boost.	Trajectory adjustments of bus and release of MIRVs and Penaids.	Free ballistic flight of MIRVs and Penaids.	MIRVs and Penaids re-enter atmosphere.
	Rocket exhaust detection. Intercept by space DEWs	Intercept by space DEWs.	Early intercept by space DEWs — Later intercept by long-range ABMs.	Layered intercept by short-range ABMs and ground DEWs.

Stage 1
Stage 2
Stage 3 (Early)
Stage 4
Surveillance Satellite

ABM
MIRVS
Penaids

Phase 1
Phase 2
Phase 3
Phase 4
Stage 3 (Later)

Altitude (km)
1200
200
100 (Limit of atmosphere)
10,000 km
Distance

warheads it released. If only a percentage are going to penetrate a defence they will increase massively the number of missiles and warheads and seek to swamp the defence. This leads on to a third point. To be effective a defensive shield would have to be totally effective. If 1,000 warheads are released and the system is 95 per cent effective, that means 50 warheads get through, and that means massive devastation. Fourthly, even if there was a totally effective defensive shield in space, that would provide no defence against systems that operate in the atmosphere, such as bombers and cruise missiles. It would be like repairing the roof and leaving the doors and windows open. Fifthly, a defensive shield in space would be destabilizing. If a fully operational defensive shield ever was developed, it would be a temptation for the state that sheltered under it to think it could fight a nuclear war and survive without destroying itself. Even more crucial, before such a system ever came to be deployed, it might tempt the side that felt behind with technology to strike whilst there was still a chance of a strike being effective. It is true that there have been suggestions of an exchange of technology, so that both sides would develop a shield at the same rate. But a more likely move would be a competitive and asymmetric scramble to be the first to achieve a comprehensive shield.

There is, of course, a case in favour of SDI. Apart from the ethical arguments about the desirability of defence rather than deterrence, which will be considered later, it is argued that even a partially effective defence is better than no defence at all; that such a defence would not only limit the danger of a major attack, but would also provide an effective defence against the missiles of a small power like Libya or against the accidental release of a missile. Further, it is pointed out that the Soviet Union has its own SDI research programme, which is true, and it is only prudent to investigate a promising line of research which offers hope for the future. Finally it is pointed out that what is being discussed is research not deployment.

However, these arguments, even when taken together, seem little enough to pit against the almost overwhelming objections outlined earlier. Yet SDI clearly has an appeal and it has already developed a powerful momentum. One of the reasons for this is that it holds out the hope of a switch to a more defensive system. *The Times,* which has led the popular defence of SDI in Europe wrote, in its leader of 19 September 1984:

> In principle, it must be right to prefer a defensive system, albeit an imperfect one, than to continue with the arid menace of mutual assured destruction.

Again on 25 September 1984 it said:

> The experience of the last twenty-five years should have convinced us all of the folly of predicting confidently what will or will not be technically possible in five or ten years' time. It is surely common prudence to determine through a programme of serious scientific enquiry, whether it is possible to shift the balance of advantage between offensive and defensive systems and so move away from the crude calculus of 'mutual assured destruction'.

First a comment needs to be made about the phrase 'mutual assured destruction'. For this can be a deliberate strategy or a risk of any strategy in the nuclear age. As already discussed, it is possible to have an effective deterrence system that does not depend on a policy of total destruction, and for moral reasons such a policy should be eschewed. But mutual assured destruction is an inescapable risk of the nuclear age, in the sense that there are enough nuclear weapons in existence to kill the inhabitants of the earth several times over. And, without massive reductions in arms, this would still be so even with a defensive shield in space. For, as President Reagan admitted in his speech of 23 March 1983, during the construction of such a shield there could be no question of moving away from a policy of nuclear deterrence. Nor, as has emerged since that speech, would there really be much prospect of moving away from it afterwards. Even if the defensive shield were fully operational, the threat of unacceptable destruction would still be central to the relationship of the two superpowers. As Elizabeth Young has put it,

'It would, however, be at an indefinitely higher level of expense, and of risk and of irrelevance'.

So there is no real possibility of getting back to the defensive system that prevailed in the pre-nuclear age. Even with a shield in space, deterrence would still be fundamental. The stress that this is only a research programme also needs to be questioned. Research programmes build up their own momentum, so that testing (which in any case is difficult to disassociate from research) and deployment follow all too easily, particularly where jobs are at stake and money is to be made.

The secular arguments, then, against the development of SDI are formidable. But are there any special Christian considerations to bring to bear on the issue? First, it is important to challenge what might be called the argument from momentum, which suggests that the development of SDI is inevitable so we may as well 'get in on the act' from the beginning and see that we obtain our share of the research contracts. It is easy to see how an 'it's inevitable' frame of mind can build up. Over recent centuries and in particular recent decades, technology has proceeded apace. Every new development in military technology, the longbow, the crossbow, gunpowder, the machine gun, bombs and atomic weapons have been greeted with moral condemnation: to no avail. It is difficult to imagine that nuclear weapons, terrible though they are, represent the end of the road. Then, the desire of human beings to dominate every new sphere of potential warfare seems as strong as its desire to advance technologically. War was carried from the land on to the sea and then under the sea. War was carried from the land and into the air. War in space, above the atmosphere, seems the next inevitable step. As always with things human, good and ill are inextricably mixed together. Military technology is closely bound up with research for peaceful purposes and has its roots in human inventiveness. The desire to dominate every new sphere is closely linked to our human capacity to face a challenge, whether it is Everest or a four minute mile. This mixture is part of the reason why the impetus towards a new threshold in the arms race and a new form of warfare is as strong as it is. Then there is the obvious fear that the other side, whoever they are, are moving in this direction and so we must go there too in order not to be left behind. The other side might gain a crucial advantage, which it would be irresponsible to let them have. Finally there is what President Eisenhower called 'the military-industrial complex'. The US budget for the limited first five year programme of SDI research is $56 billion. This means jobs and profits for a great number of people.

The argument that SDI is inevitable was put by Lord Chalfont in an article in *The Times* on 19 August 1985:

> It may be, of course, that European governments, concerned about their own nuclear systems, about arms control, and about American hegemony, will stand aside from the Strategic Defence Initiative. If they do, they must calculate the eventual cost, since one thing is certain. If the United States government cannot count on the collaboration of its European allies, it will go ahead without it. So, whatever NATO does, will the Soviet Union.

So the argument from momentum can itself build up and provide a formidable rolling stock. But it must be stopped. Human beings are free, and technology is not a force with a will of its own. Technology is a tool of humanity and needs to be treated as such.

The second specifically Christian consideration is related to the original vision put forward by President Reagan for the justification of SDI research. In his speech of 23 March 1983 President Reagan said:

> I have become more and more deeply convinced that the human spirit must be capable of rising above dealing with other nations and human beings by threatening their existence . . . let me share with you a vision of the future which offers hope. It is that we embark on a program to counter the awesome soviet missile threat with measures that are defensive. . . . What if free people could live secure in the knowledge that their security did not rest upon the threat of instant US retali-

ation to deter a soviet attack; that we could intercept and
destroy strategic ballistic missiles before they reached
our own soil or that of our allies. . . . There will be
failures and setbacks. . . . But is it not worth every
investment necessary to free the world from the threat
of nuclear war? We know it is . . . I call upon the scientific community who gave us nuclear weapons to turn
their great talents to the cause of mankind and world
peace; to give us the means of rendering these nuclear
weapons impotent and obsolete.

There is no doubt that this speech, in which President Reagan
made a personal contribution that took many of his officials
by surprise, has a moral appeal. It made a major impact and
was supported by the great majority of the American people
particularly in the crucial period of voting funds for SDI
research, though by the end of 1985 that support had fallen
considerably. The speech has what seems to be a deeply felt
personal moral thrust which, as we have seen, has appealed to
the editor of *The Times* in such a way as to override other
criticisms. In the aftermath of the announcement of the SDI
research programme, as it became increasingly clear that there
could probably never be such a thing as a leak-proof
astrodome in space, modified versions were put forward, in
particular the idea that a point defence should be developed,
rather than a more comprehensive one. In other words
ballistic missile defence should be developed for missile
emplacements. It has been argued that, if both superpowers
developed this more limited BMD, deterrence would be
enhanced, for all the ICBMs of both powers would then be
secure from a crippling first-strike attack. Nevertheless,
Secretary of Defence Caspar Weinberger, in a speech on 1
May 1984, affirmed that the original version still stands:

The ultimate goal of the strategic defence initiative is to
develop thoroughly reliable defences. This does not
preclude of course any intermediate deployment. . . .
Those intermediate capabilities are completely consis-
tent with the ultimate goal.

It is the thought of 'thoroughly reliable defences' that makes the appeal. In President Reagan's ringing phrases: 'Is it not worth every investment necessary to free the world from the threat of nuclear war. . . . I call upon the scientific community to give us the means of rendering these nuclear weapons impotent and obsolete.'

The various reasons why this vision is highly unlikely to be fulfilled have already been listed, the virtual impossibility of shooting down every single one of thousands of incoming missiles; the relative ease with which counter measures could be taken by a potential attacker; the continuing problem of air breathing weapons like cruise and aircraft borne nuclear devices. But there is a still more fundamental point that must be raised. The desire for a totally secure defence in this life is a mirage. The threat of nuclear war is here to stay for the forseeable future. Human beings are vulnerable in a threatening world. This is the daily reality for most of mankind, faced as they are with famine, drought, flood, natural disaster and communal violence. In the West we are to some extent protected from these things. It is easy to slip into the assumption that we really are secure or if there is some area of our life where we are at present vulnerable, if only enough scientific effort and money was put into remedying the situation we could achieve total security. But there is no ultimate security through human endeavour. Part of the appeal of SDI as put forward by President Reagan is that it appeals to man's age-old longing for total security. But absolute security is not available on this earth, certainly not in an age with weapons of an unlimited destructive power. This does not, of course, preclude responsible steps to achieve as much security as can reasonably be had. But the US President offered more than that. He held out the vision of a world freed from the nuclear threat. It was this that appealed in his speech. But this is utopianism and like all utopianism, dangerous. SDI is an attempt at a technological fix for a human and political problem — our propensity to fight. Such problems can hardly ever be solved in that way. We have to address real causes in the terms really relevant to them.

There is, thirdly, another theological error lurking behind the development of SDI, one related to the desire for total security. Throughout human history human beings have sought the high ground. All over Britain you can see Iron Age castles, a hill with a flat top for pasture surrounded by a ditch and double bank; all over the world you can see stone castles, often built on the edge of precipitous cliffs to make them even more able to dominate the countryside around them. When battles began in World War 2 troops sought the high ground from which, again, they could dominate the enemy. Space is the ultimate high ground. It has been argued by some that there are certain high orbits in which satellites could be placed which would be able to dominate all warfare for ever. This is the final frontier, the ultimate high ground. But there is clearly something highly suspect in this continuing attempt to reach high ground so that dominance over all other groups can be achieved and, through that dominance, security for oneself. There is no security through dominance and the attempt to reach the ultimate high ground can only be seen as an act of hubris.

It was suggested in Chapter Three that the continual warring of human beings was not simply a result of a contribution of our animal nature but that it arose in part because we are spiritual as well as animal. Through dominating others we put ourselves at the centre; and so it is that the will-to-survive becomes changed, in us, to the will-to-power. This will-to-dominate, through reaching a totally dominating position, is seen with stark clarity in the attempt to dominate all space.

In addition to the development of SDI there is important and closely related research going on into anti-satellite weapons (ASATs) which also needs to be considered. Some people talk about the militarization of space. This is misleading, because space is already militarized, in that there are hundreds, if not thousands, of satellites in space serving vital military functions. They are also vital from the point of view of arms control and deterrence. First, they are crucial from an arms-control point of view, because they offer a way of verifying at least some arms-control agreements without the necessity of on-site inspection (which the USSR so dislikes). These satellites, together with the highly sophisticated equipment available for interpreting photographs, make it possible, for example, to see the difference, from space, between an ordinary saloon car and a Volkswagen Beetle. So it is possible to monitor at least some agreements by these national technical means. Secondly, these satellites are crucial for deterrence. Because of their surveillance capability they are able to spot both the deployment and use of weapons. This helps to counter any tendency to strike first at the other side's weapons system. For, if you have no idea when or where the other person is likely to fire a missile, there is a temptation to hit his silos before he can fire. But if you have an assured second strike capacity, which both sides have, together with the means of detecting anything that fires, not only do you know what is going on, the enemy knows that you know. Because he knows that you would know, he is inhibited from firing a missile in the first place. Thirdly, they are vital, at least for the USA, for war fighting. Something like 90 per cent of their command, control and communications capability is in satellites. So a threat to these satellites is also a threat to deterrence and an assurance that these satellites are in place and secure, is also an enhancement of deterrence. So space is already militarized. But the functions that these satellites perform of surveillance, reconnaissance and command, control and communications, C (3), help stability and reassurance.

For this reason, therefore, the development of anti-satellite weapons must also be regarded as destabilizing and an ominous extension of the arms race. The Soviet Union has had an Asat capability for some time. It consists of a large satellite which can be launched into low-earth orbit (1,000 miles) by a version of the SS 19 ICBM. It is designed to go into orbit alongside the target satellite and destroy it with either conventional or nuclear warheads. However, the technical problems of attacking early-warning and communication satellites in geostationary orbit (22,500 miles) are formidable and it is not at all certain whether the Soviet Union is yet capable of doing this.

The United States has recently taken steps to develop its own Asat system. This is a two-stage rocket, carried to about 80,000 feet by an F-15 aircraft and capable of launching a miniature homing vehicle with an electronic locking device which carries it on a direct collision course with the target satellite. It was first tested in January of 1984.

Asat systems are different from, but related to the SDI. They are related in the sense that, if satellites were placed in space as part of a multi-layered ballistic missile defence system, they would become obvious targets for anti-satellite weapons. Furthermore, although present Asats are relatively primitive and launched from the earth, unless agreements are reached, they will almost certainly lead to more advanced weapons based in space. Asats are related to the whole move to place weapons systems in space. They are also, as I have suggested, an even more fundamental threat to both arms control and deterrence.

At present, research into both Asat weapons and SDI is at an early stage. In 1984, President Reagan set up the Strategic Defence Initiative Office (SDIO) under Lt-Gen James Abrahamson, with the job of monitoring research and reporting to the President and Congress some time in the 1990s with a recommendation whether or not to deploy such defence. So far, they have submitted one report to Caspar Weinberger, the Defence Secretary. The report shows research proceeding apace in every area connected with the SDI. It is still far too early, however, to be able to make a technical judgement about the eventual feasibility of the President's original scheme. But whatever the technical feasibility, deterrence will remain the basic fact about the relationship between the superpowers. For all the reasons suggested in this chapter the way forward should lie with achieving deterrence at mutually acceptable lower levels, not by seeking a way out of deterrence altogether, which is not possible. Behind the dream that it is possible and that this is the way to go, lie lurking, as we have suggested, some fundamental errors which the Christian faith reveals in their true colours.

Whether there is any political will in either side to achieve an agreement banning all weapons in space remains to be seen. The Soviet Union has presented the draft of a possible treaty to the UN and, when I attended a conference on weapons in space in Moscow in April 1984, the Soviet Union were clearly very anxious to obtain an agreement on both SDI and Asat weapons. In the summer of 1984, overtures were made to the USA, who seemed to respond; but then it suddenly emerged that each side appeared to the other to have laid down pre-conditions for talks which were unacceptable. Since then strategic arms talks have started in Geneva. The United States has always insisted that SDI research is not negotiable and that they are going ahead with it, whatever happens. So, no doubt, is the Soviet Union. It is still possible, however, to reach some kind of agreement before any deployment takes place. And such agreement will certainly be necessary if the 1972 treaty on ABM defence is not to be broken unilaterally.

During the 1960s limited defences against ballistic missiles looked feasible and there were many who argued that it was right to deploy them. But, in a rare moment of sanity, the USSR and the USA signed the ABM treaty cutting off this line of development and limiting defences to one on each side. It was a dramatic recognition that in the nuclear age there is no way back from deterrence to defence. The 1972 ABM treaty set a precedent which can and must be followed. It is not inevitable, even at this stage, that we go down the SDI road. And there are good reasons why we should not. Research is taking place both in the USA and the USSR. Research is very difficult to verify. What is needed is further clarification of the boundaries between research and testing on the one hand and testing and deployment on the other, followed by a ringing reaffirmation of the 1972 ABM treaty. This would not stop research but it would preclude testing and deployment.

It was part of President Reagan's original vision of SDI that research and technology should be shared with the Soviet Union. For obvious reasons, this point has hardly been to the fore of the debate since then, and is in danger of being lost sight of. But such sharing of research and technology, if carried out, would be a genuinely confidence-building measure.

CHAPTER THIRTEEN

Honour and hope in a nuclear world

Human history is a history of war; or so it often seems. The story of almost every land is one of invasions and repulsions, conquests and defeats, of armies advancing and being pushed back. And in the air can still be heard the screams from countless cruel deaths, unspeakable tortures and hideous brutalities; the ghastly, pitiable, suffering of unknown millions. The ruins of Troy are formed from the stones of twelve cities that have been erected and razed on the same site; and that is only one city in one continent.

Most of us now view warfare with an outlook shaped by Wilfred Owen's experience of the first World War. We see only tragic, futile, pitiful waste. We react against many of the old notions of patriotism, honour and sacrifice for one's country in war. It is prudent, however, to be as alert to the almost instinctive nature of our present attitude to war as we are critical of the unthinking jingoism of so many before 1914. We, no less than they, are subject to historical forces and cultural changes. More important, from a Christian point of view, is it right to consign so much endeavour and suffering to the dustbin marked 'futility'? For the Christian is concerned not only with the ethics of war but also with the redemption of God's creatures; and it is difficult to see how there can be any redemption beyond space and time unless we can see some soul of good in things in space and time, however tragic, futile or even evil they may appear. Professor Michael Howard has said:

> The trouble is that if Christianity really is incompatible with war, we have to turn our backs on two thousand years of warring Christendom and assume that during those centuries God was unaccountably withholding His Holy Spirit from His Church. No: God can only

work *through* his creation; and His Church consists of men and women who are not so much sinful (for . . . wars do not come about just because we are sinful) as shaped by their history and culture. . . . The Church is inexorably *part* of its background, of the society around it. It reflects and expresses the changing values and the conflicts of that society. God did not give any of us the power to transcend the cultural limits of our own times. He finds us as we are, and uses us as He sees fit. In His house are many mansions, and there is plenty of room for the warrior priest as well as the Quaker, for the crusader for war as well as the crusader for peace.[1]

In the end, war is part of the whole process of how evil and suffering are to be reconciled with the purposes of a loving creator, a question which takes us beyond the scope of this book.[2] But this at least must be said: in war, as in every other circumstance, God is ceaselessly at work bringing some unique good out of the evil that has come to pass. So it has been that, whilst some have sunk lower than the beasts, millions of people caught up in wars and revolutions have been raised beyond themselves. Forced, like all human beings, to work out their destiny within a particular historical context, with only limited room for manoeuvre, they have shown courage, nobility and pity. Standing by the walls of Troy a Homeric scholar has said:

> The Trojan War was a 'Great War' with all the brutality and futility implied by that label. But when tragically caught up in such conflicts men and women can rise above their normal selves to a higher nobility of thought and action. Out of the double bereavement can come the reconciliation of a Priam and an Achilles. Homer does not spare us the horror and anguish of battle, but neither does he despair of human nature. He has shown us what human beings at their most human can do, and must suffer.[3]

Homer's *Iliad,* Europe's first and, in the judgement of some, still its greatest classic, is poignant and salutary reading for all

those who reflect on war. It brings out three points of
particular importance. First, human beings are in large
measure moved by forces outside their control. Homer
depicts this in terms of the gods. It is a quarrel between the
gods and what the gods do to help or hinder the battle, that
brings good fortune or bad, and which causes powerful
victory to lurch from one side to the other; and perhaps the
gods themselves are subject to fate. We do not think like that.
But if we think of human beings atomistically, each individual struggling with his or her own decisions in isolation,
we miss an important dimension of the truth. For the ancient
Greeks possessed a tragic sense, a knowledge that we are *to
some extent* at the mercy of larger forces. In Edward Thomas's
moving poem 'As the team's Head-Brass', the poet sits on an
elm blown down in a storm and talks to the ploughman as he
turns round the corner. The ploughman comments:

> 'Only two teams work on the farm this year.
> One of my mates is dead. The second day
> In France they killed him. It was back in March,
> The very night of the blizzard too. Now if
> He had stayed here we should have moved the tree.'
> 'And I should not have sat here. Everything
> Would have been different. For it would have been
> Another world.' 'Ay, and a better, though
> If we could see all all might seem good.'[4]

It is a poem that well captures the uniqueness of a particular
moment within the context of vast disruptive forces that have
made it what it is. Secondly, though our circumstances are
shaped by factors outside our control, so that too often young
people have had their lives tragically cut short in war, yet
even within war there are moments of grace. In one of the
most profound meditations on the *Iliad,* written after the fall
of France in 1940, Simone Weil sees force itself as a something
almost tangible and as one of the strongest elements that drive
our destiny. Force turns people into things. Yet the *Iliad* does
more than reveal this happening. For Simone Weil sees:

> this bitterness that proceeds from tenderness and that
> spreads over the whole human race, impartial as

sunlight. Nothing precious is scorned, whether or not death is its destiny; everyone's unhappiness is laid bare without dissimulation or disdain; no man is set above or below the condition common to all men; whatever is destroyed is regretted.[5]

To say that there are large impersonal forces at work in human history is in no way to undermine the necessity of making ethical decisions about war or within war. Perhaps we will be led to have nothing to do with war and become a pacifist or, like Simone Weil herself, under no illusions, to support the French Resistance against the Nazis. But inescapably our destiny is worked out within a context of force and either way there is the tenderness implicit in the *Iliad*:

This poem is a miracle. Its bitterness is the only justifiable bitterness for it springs from the subjection of the human spirit to force, that is, in the last analysis, to matter. This subjection is the common lot, although each spirit will bear it differently, in proportion to its own virtue. No one in the *Iliad* is spared by it, as no one on earth is. No one who succumbs to it is by virtue of this fact regarded with contempt. Whoever, within his own soul and in human relations, escapes the dominion of force is loved but loved sorrowfully because of the threat of destruction that constantly hangs over him.[6]

Thirdly, for all the emphasis within the *Iliad* on fate and despite the unremitting violence, there is another value present, which we can only call honour. In the *Iliad,* it does not in the end matter whether a person lives or dies, for we all die anyway and fate has appointed the time. What does matter is that we live with honour and die properly honoured. Hence, what is to us amazing, the agonized fight over the body of Patroclus. One side wants the body in order to ravage and dishonour it, the other to give it an honoured burial. Hence the visit of King Priam to Achilles to recover the body of his son Hector, which Achilles has been doing his best to disfigure and dishonour. We find this stress on proper honour to a corpse strange: but it expresses a profound truth.

There is something more important at stake in life than merely living or dying.

These wider considerations derived from the *Iliad* are crucial because, if human history is a history of war, the Christian looks for that within war which is capable of redemption or is a sign of redemption. Nor is it only history that is a story of wars; wars are taking place all over the world at the moment. Since the second World War there have been nearly 150 conventional wars and over 40 million people have died in them. At the moment we have only to think of Iran and Iraq, the Lebanon, Israel and the Arabs, South Africa, Afghanistan, Central America. The list is endless and there is virtually no country in the world where there is not either a war going on or violence between the state and some minority group. In human terms this means young men, women and children caught up in conflicts not of their own making, suffering and sometimes making others suffer for what they believe to be legitimate reason. All this is but the *Iliad* spilled out over the world. But, if this reflects the *Iliad*, there is that within all war which is redeemable: no war is totally futile in the sense that within it are human beings, children of God, working out their destiny.[7]

How far, however, are these wider considerations pertinent to a nuclear age? The first two can certainly be affirmed. Human beings now, as always, are caught up in historical and cultural movements. We have to work out our destinies within the nuclear age not apart from it. Furthermore, the sense of tender pity in which the *Iliad* is bathed and which took shape in a different way in the poems of Wilfred Owen is applicable now to both the nuclear planner and CND activist.

The third point, however, brings out the gulf that separates us from those who have struggled with the problem of force in every other age. There could be no honour in a nuclear war. For, however brutally Achilles threw his spear through the jaw of an enemy or thrust his sword through his stomach, he both faced him as a person and put his own life at risk. In a missile age we neither face the enemy nor, in the way Achilles did, put out own lives on the line. In a nuclear war it would be non-combatants who would bear the brunt of the casualties, as they would in any war between the superpowers today, even if nuclear weapons were not involved. Leonard Cheshire, who was the British observer at the dropping of the atom bomb on Nagasaki, describes his feelings as the plane flew in:

> The fact that we were out of the range of the defences made me uneasy; it felt unfair. Over Germany we had suffered a permanent casualty rate of just under 5 per cent per night; the average number of trips an aircrew could hope to make was twenty-five. Whatever casualties we might be inflicting — and after all, we argued, the German workers knew we were coming; they could always have abandoned their jobs and fled the cities — we ourselves were suffering proportionately more. In an odd sort of way it felt fair, whereas this did not.[8]

For some, such considerations can have no place. Yet they bring out the basis of such honour as can be found in war. For that reason it is difficult to see how there could be any honour in a nuclear exchange launched by politicians and servicemen in hardened command posts. Honour, in a nuclear age, is to be found by so managing events that war is avoided.

The existence of the almost limitless force provided by nuclear weapons makes our age radically different from every other. It has necessitated rethinking all the old concepts of war. Some feel that our time is so different that history itself is coming to an end; history is coming to its climax in our time and the end of all things is at hand. On at least five occasions in as many years, President Reagan has referred to his belief that Armaggedon may occur in this generation and has associated this with the end of the world. Behind Reagan there lies Evangelical fundamentalism, particularly that of Jerry Falwell, leader of the so-called Moral Majority. Falwell has said that there will be a nuclear holocaust in the next sixty years. Russia will be destroyed by nuclear weapons but Christians living in Russia will be 'raptured', that is, physically transported to heaven in the twinkling of an eye.

Nor is this approach confined to American fundamentalists. In the debate of the General Synod of the Church of England on nuclear weapons in February 1983 the then

Archbishop of York, Stuart Blanche, said, 'This debate is about the end of the world and about how we may prevent or delay it'. Again, 'from now on every generation will be aware that it could be the last generation on earth'. In this context he, like others, quoted an apocalyptic saying from St Luke's Gospel, 'When you see these things come to pass, lift up your heads, for your redemption draws near'.[9]

This kind of teaching is highly dangerous, for it engenders an impression that nuclear war is inevitable and at the same time tries to make such a war religiously acceptable. It is also false to biblical teaching.[10]

Apart from the fact that the whole biblical view of man, with its stress on human freedom and responsibility, is opposed to fatalism, it implies a thoroughly parochial view of 'the end'. When the New Testament talks about 'the end' it means the goal of the universe, not simply the physical demise of this planet. Moreover, this end will be brought about by God. There is no necessary connection between a nuclear exchange and the end of all things. Furthermore, the end in Christian terms means the transmutation of this physical order into the stuff of eternity. An all out nuclear exchange, if it engulfed the whole planet, might mean the end of human life or even life itself on earth.[11] It would not of itself indicate the coming of Christ in glory and the creation of that new heaven and new earth that is mentioned in the Book of Revelation.

Another picture of the future given by the Bible is that one day the world will be rid of the scourge of war. Then:

> they shall beat their swords into ploughshares, and their spears into pruning hooks; nation shall not lift up sword against nation, neither shall they learn war any more.
> But they shall sit every man under his vine and under his fig tree; and none shall make them afraid; for the mouth of the Lord of hosts hath spoken it.[12]

How far can this vision be realized on earth?

It is necessary first to explore possible motives for arms reductions. One popular slogan says that money spent on arms deprives people in the developing world of basic necessities; money on arms is therefore killing people by starvation. But caution is needed about this kind of appeal. To begin with it is often claimed that it is the *nuclear* arms race that is depriving the poor of the world of their rights. But nuclear arms are, comparatively speaking, cheaper than modern sophisticated conventional weapons, if you are already a nuclear power. It is not so much the modernization of nuclear weapons that is the problem as the trade in conventional weapons to developing nations. This is an extremely serious and difficult problem with which the Church ought to be far more engaged. But the Churches have been over-preoccupied with the nuclear issue. Certainly if the money spent on arms is the main concern it is with conventional arms that one ought to begin.[13] Another point is that defence and third-world development are not simple alternatives. The former, in proper measure, may be a precondition of the latter. If during the 1930s we had spent even less on defence and so lost to Hitler, poverty and starvation would not have been better alleviated. This is true not only in the relationship between the developed and the developing world but, more tragically, in the developing world itself. Developing countries, however poor, have necessary and legitimate security needs, which unless they are adequately catered for, can result in anarchic disruption and total breakdown of the administrative machinery: which is why the problem of arms sales is no more simple than any other, urgent though it is to achieve agreements in this area.

The other reason for caution about the appeal to turn arms into bread is that it could imply that nothing much can be done about the starving until arms production has been slowed down. But the moral claim of the starving on us exists in its own right. It is to be responded to now, whatever arms are being produced. Nor is it a shortage of resources that is hindering the help properly due to the poorest of the earth. The resources are there, the food is there. It would be a pity if the claimed connection between arms and food blunted people's sensitivity to a problem that can and ought to be tackled now, for its own sake, whatever other money might be spent on arms.

Another possible motive for working for arms reductions

is that their presence makes the world highly unsafe and we would all be much more secure without them. This is not the position taken in this book. Nuclear deterrence is fundamentally robust. We must therefore so manage any arms reductions that can be agreed in such a way that the world does not become more unstable as a result.

The proper Christian motive in working for arms reductions is quite simply that a world bristling with arms is a standing denial of that perfect society, the kingdom of God, which Jesus put before us in his teaching and which he inaugurated on earth through his life, death and resurrection. In that society we live without defences of any kind, with total trust in God and completely vulnerable to one another. It was one of the themes of earlier chapters of this book that the vision of this society given by Jesus is one of the two poles of Christian truth; and that it lives in tension with the duties of civil society necessitated by an imperfect world. This picture of the kingdom both judges our political arrangements, revealing them for what they are, compromises made necessary by human sin, and beckons us to make the vision a reality, as far as we can under the conditions of a flawed and finite human existence. The pole of Christian truth provided by Jesus's ethic of the kingdom is in no way to be pushed aside. It is there as an absolute standard over every human arrangement, seeking, so far as it can, to permeate and modify those arrangements. We saw, for example, how people like Suarez and Grotius, who would be regarded as belonging to the Christian realist camp, nevertheless allowed considerations of charity to impinge upon and influence political and military decisions. It is a vision of the kingdom, this new order of divine charity, that impels us to work for a world less reliant on armaments.

But how do we bring about this very different world? In recent years many people have stressed the role of arms in making the world a hostile and unsafe place. But arms express political realities. Change the political realities for the better and arms are no longer necessary; or, if they still exist, they are not felt as a threat. Are the British frightened by the French nuclear force? They are not frightened because, on the whole, reasonable political relationships exist between the two countries, even though, in the past, we have often been at war with one another. The first priority therefore in relationships between the West and the Soviet Union is to achieve better political relationships. Without this, little will be possible in the way of arms reductions; with this better relationship, arms reductions will appear natural. It is true that modernization of weapons can appear a threat, as the placing of SS 20s by the Soviet Union did to NATO and as Pershing II did to the Soviet Union. But, more fundamentally, weapons are a sign of the disease, not a cause of it. Under certain circumstances they can make the disease worse, as when a boil goes septic. But the fact that there is a boil there at all is because there is something wrong with the bloodstream.

In trying to bring about a different, better, world the Church needs to be characterized by both a sense of urgency and a sense of perspective. The urgency has nothing to do with the frenetic panic engendered by those who think that nuclear disaster is round the corner. The urgency is a Christian urgency springing from the absolute claims of the kingdom of God, which impinge upon us at every moment calling us to respond to them, so far as we can in our circumstances. But a longer perspective is no less important. It took many centuries for Catholics and Protestants to learn to share the same Europe without killing one another (and even now they have not quite achieved it). Now, once again, we live in a world dominated by two radically opposed ideologies. Neither side is suddenly going to renounce its ideology. Eventually they must learn to live together in the same world without threatening one another's existence. This process of gradual adaptation and modification may take a long time. Mutual and balanced arms reductions will be both a sign that this process is happening and also one, but only one, of the ways in which it is brought about.

How far will we be able to go down the road towards general and complete disarmament? In one sense we must go right to the end of the road, for the kingdom of God is characterized by general and complete disarmament. Nothing less than that must satisfy us. But we can neither say that the vision of that society will be realized on this earth, nor deny that it will. It remains as the absolute standard, hovering over every moment, and will do so to the end of time. It beckons to us to realize it within time, but we will never be in a position to predict when and how it will be realized, any more than Jesus himself was in that position.

This vision of a society lived in total trust on God and with complete openness to one another is not a utopia. Utopias are either fantasies that have no basis in reality or else dreams that people think can be made realities if all the ordinary features of life are ignored. The kingdom of God differs from utopias both in being grounded in reality, indeed, in *being* the ultimate reality, and also by living in tension with, rather than ignoring, political realities. The situation can be brought home in a parable.

President Reagan and Mr Gorbachov are walking together in the woods. In some ways the world is rather different from what it is now. Relationships between the superpowers have improved and all other nuclear weapons in the world have been dismantled. The two superpowers themselves have reduced their military arsenals to a genuinely minimum deterrent. They retain some conventional forces and also a nuclear component able to inflict unacceptable damage to the other side. In other respects, however, the world has not changed. The two sides both believe in their ideologies, the states system still exists, and human nature has not changed. Should the two powers take a final step and divest themselves of the nuclear component in their military arsenals? It is not obvious they should. On the one hand there is the ethic of greater trust. On the other hand there is the age-old reality of potential imperialism which is held in check by that nuclear component. Could we risk moving into a world in which once again there would be no overarching brake on war? The Christian cannot say in advance that it would be wrong to do so. But equally, as we look from the perspective where we are now, it is certainly not obvious that we should take that risk.

Nuclear weapons are very terrible weapons of destruction. Yet it would be dishonest to deny that they have brought about one major benefit. For the first time in human history it could not be in the interest of a major power to go to war against another power that possessed nuclear weapons.

Nuclear war is not a rational option. In this, some of us would see the hand of God using our evil intentions for good purposes.[14] The nuclear threat hangs over us as a warning of the cost of going to war. In this is a divine judgement forcing states to be prudent and cautious; to find ways, other than war, of resolving their disputes. So there is a strange mercy in nuclear deterrence, but it lives in tension with the hope of the kingdom of God, that perfect society in which neither war nor deterrence will be any more. That society has its origins and destiny beyond space and time but it has to be built up, worked for and worked towards within time and space.

Notes

1. The University Sermon, delivered at St Mary the Virgin, Oxford, on 11 November 1984 by Professor Michael Howard, Regius Professor of Modern History in the University of Oxford.
2. I have tried to say something on the subject in Chapter Five of *Being a Christian,* Mowbray, 1981.
3. Talk at Troy by Professor J.V. Luce, Professor of Greek, Trinity College, Dublin, in May 1985.
4. 'As the team's Head-Brass' in Edward Thomas, *Collected Poems,* Faber, 1974, p.29.
5. Simone Weil, *The Iliad or The Poem of Force,* Pendle Hill, Pennsylvania, pp.29–30.
6. Ibid, p.33.
7. The sense of human beings caught up in great events over which they have little control was classically stated by Tolstoy in *War and Peace.* Evelyn Waugh makes the same point, satirically, in his *Sword of Honour* trilogy. Laurens Van der Post, a prisoner of the Japanese, shows how this sense can be related to compassion for the individual. In *The Night of the New Moon* he related how he was made to watch bayonet practice on live prisoners of war and other barbarities. This made him feel that dark forces had invaded the Japanese spirit. 'It was, indeed, the awareness of this dark invasion which made it impossible for us to have any personal feelings against our captors, because it made us realise how the Japanese themselves were the puppets of immense impersonal forces to such an extent that they truly did not know what they were doing.'

8. Leonard Cheshire, *The Light of Many Suns,* Methuen, 1985, p.55.
9. Luke 21.28.
10. See the good article by the Bishop of Salisbury (John Austin Baker) 'Theology and Nuclear Weapons', *King's Theological Review,* Spring 1983, Vol.VI, No.1.
11. Jonathan Schell, *The Fate of the Earth,* Jonathan Cape, 1982.
12. Micah 4.3-4. See also Isaiah 2.4 and Joel 3.10.
13. The most comprehensive analysis of the situation and its difficulties is Andrew Pierre, *The Global Politics of Arms Sales,* Princeton, 1982. See also Peter Blomley, 'The Arms Trade and Arms Conversion' in *Armed Peace,* ed. Josephine O'Conner Howe, Macmillan, 1984.
14. I have developed this point in 'The Strange Mercy of Deterrence' in *Dropping the Bomb.*